A GUIDE TO
CAVES AND KARST OF INDIANA

INDIANA NATURAL SCIENCE

Gillian Harris, editor

A GUIDE TO
CAVES AND KARST
OF INDIANA

SAMUEL S. FRUSHOUR
IN CONJUNCTION WITH THE
INDIANA GEOLOGICAL SURVEY

WITH A CONTRIBUTION BY
JULIAN J. LEWIS AND SALISA L. LEWIS

INDIANA UNIVERSITY PRESS
Bloomington & Indianapolis

This book is a publication of

Indiana University Press
601 North Morton Street
Bloomington, Indiana 47404-3797 USA

iupress.indiana.edu

Telephone orders   800-842-6796
Fax orders   812-855-7931

Printed in China

Library of Congress Cataloging-in-Publication Data

Frushour, Samuel S.
A guide to caves and karst of Indiana / Samuel S. Frushour ;
with a contribution by Julian J. Lewis and Salisa L. Lewis.
p.   cm. — (Indiana natural science)
Includes bibliographical references and index.
ISBN 978-0-253-00096-5 (pbk. : alk. paper) 1. Caves—Indiana—
Guidebooks. 2. Karst—Indiana—Guidebooks. I. Title.
GB605.I6F78   2012
551.44'709772—dc23   2012001568

1   2   3   4   5   17   16   15   14   13   12

CONTENTS

CONTENTS

A GUIDE TO
CAVES AND KARST OF INDIANA

Plate 1. Cave visitors may encounter: (A) water crawls in streams; (B) tight squeezes for the caver to negotiate; (C) enchanting scenes in some Indiana caves; (D) a large borehole passageway; (E) a canyon passageway where climbing is required; (F) rainwater that may pour into swallow holes to flood many caves.
PHOTOS BY SAMUEL S. FRUSHOUR.

Introduction

With more than 3,000 known caves in the state of Indiana, it is not surprising that humans have used them for a variety of purposes. Aboriginal peoples used caves as shelter and as a resource for raw materials (Munson and Munson 1990). Early settlers found the fresh water issuing from spring caves to be an important source of drinking water and a source of power for grist mills for making corn meal and flour. Even today, some residents of southern Indiana consume water from caves where there are no surface streams or wells are not practical. The cool water and air in caves could chill and preserve food products. A few caves were mined for soil and rock from which saltpeter was leached for making gunpowder.

In more recent years, caves have become the sites of scientific investigations, as well as places of recreation. Geologists, biologists, and hydrologists study caves as natural laboratories. Environmental researchers study cave streams and sediments to measure the effects of agricultural and industrial activities. And as we have enjoyed an increase in leisure time, so an increasing number of individuals have discovered the recreational use of caves, either by visiting commercial tour caves or exploring wild caves.

In this publication, we describe several Indiana caves. A number of commercial caves are open for public visitation and charge an admission price. However, most of Indiana's caves are located on private property and require permission from the owner for access. Certain caves on public lands, forests, and parks also require the visitor to secure permission from county, state, or federal agencies. Above all, cave visitors must remember that they are guests and should respect the property and wishes of the cave owners. We must carefully protect caves from damage to preserve these delicate natural resources for future generations.

What Is a Cave?

Caves are places of mystery and are often the subject of local legends and folktales. The moment one experiences solid bedrock overhead, an entirely new and awesome world is encountered (plate 1). *Cave* can be used to describe a dim region under a rock overhang, or thousands of feet of tortuous passageways under the surface of the land. Caves are naturally occurring cavities, and humans seem to have a natural curiosity about them. Just peering into the darkness within a cave entrance frequently sparks a desire to know what lies inside and what creatures may live there. According to local legends, several courthouses in southern Indiana have a cave running directly underneath them. Just ask a person in rural Indiana about caves and you will surely hear exaggerated tales of bats, snakes, and bottomless pits. And if allowed to enter a privately owned cave, you may be reminded, "Don't get fast in the hole."

Visitors to commercial or tourist caves are usually told that the cave was formed by an underground river. The visitor may wonder how a river could produce passageways that go up and down, get larger and smaller, have dead ends, and sometimes form intersecting networks. No stream on the surface of the earth behaves in such a manner—nor do underground rivers and streams. The enlargement of underground fractures into caves leads to other processes, such as collapse of rock and sedimentation; these processes create caves and make each individual cave an interesting and unique place to visit.

FORMATION
OF INDIANA CAVES

Caves are continually undergoing a process of change. Changes underground that relate to cave development are the enlargement of fractures, joints, and cave passages through dissolution of bedrock and the transport of coarse- and fine-grained sediments by moving water. Along with the underground processes that result in transport and deposition of cave sediments, sinkholes, swallow holes, and cave entrances on the ground surface allow water or gravity to transport soil, rocks, and organic materials into underground spaces; these also become sediments in cave passages.

Caves are formed by the chemical and physical action of water. Limestone (calcium carbonate) is the most prevalent substance in which caves are formed; it is dissolved at varying rates by the action of rainwater and water from snow melt. Precipitation absorbs some carbon dioxide from the air or soil through which it passes to become slightly acidic groundwater containing carbonic acid. This carbonic acid can dissolve limestone (fig. 1) (Palmer 2007).

Other rock layers interbedded with limestone, such as dolomite (calcium-magnesium-carbonate), gypsum (calcium-sulfate), and calcareous shale, are also subject to the action of water. Solution is concentrated along joints, or cracks, in the bedrock and in some instances may also enlarge bedding planes that separate one bed of rock from another. Joints often develop in sets that may run approximately parallel with subordinate joints, more or less at right angles, with the result that some caves show right-angle or maze patterns (Powell 1976). Subordinate joints often pass through one or more beds of stone resulting in caves that have a sinuous or random-appearing pattern, but solution along joints typically dominates the direction and shape of cave passages. The cave formation process is enhanced by the eroding effects of sand and gravel suspended in

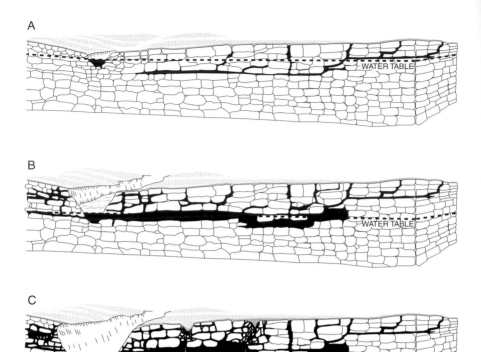

Figure 1. Cavern development results from the lowering of groundwater base level by erosion and valley deepening by surface streams with the result of increased hydraulic gradient and downward flow of groundwater. (A) Initial downcutting of surface streams lowers the water table allowing soil water to infiltrate soluble bedrock and initiate dissolution. (B) Additional lowering of surface streams promotes extensive subsurface dissolution and cave development. (C) Underground streams may abandon passages as base level of surface streams is lowered by erosion (idealized diagrams).

Figure 2. Cross-sections illustrating progressive enlargement of conduits and caves. (A) Dissolution along joints and bedding plane partings below the water table. (B) Dissolution enlargement of small conduits by storm waters. (C) Development of a cave with sediments and a free-flowing stream. (D) Development of a canyon passage by dissolution and erosion with deposition of dripstone in the air-filled passage. (E) Additional enlargement and deposition of dripstone. (F) Widening of the channel with collapse of wall rock. DRAWING BY R. L. POWELL.

4

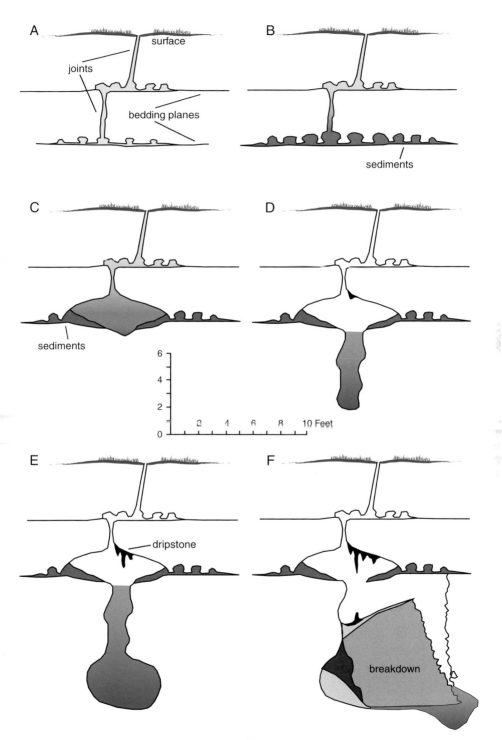

A
surface
joints
bedding planes

B
sediments

C
sediments

D
6
4
2
0
2   4   6   8   10 Feet

E
dripstone

F
dripstone
breakdown

5

storm waters that travel through the cave. Once water flow has reached sufficient velocity that particles are transported, abrasion of the rock surface augments the solution process.

Cave development may begin both above and within the underground zone of groundwater saturation. The surfaces of the bedrock in joints, fractures, and, in places, bedding planes are dissolved to evolve into conduits and caves capable of transmitting water (fig. 2). Seasonal changes in groundwater level and velocity affect cave development (Palmer 2007). During periods of low groundwater level, water flows freely by gravity as a small stream with only limited rock surface affected, while in periods of high water and increased velocity, the voids and fractures can be totally inundated; this results in solution on all available bedrock surfaces.

The joints that dominate cave passage development and the location of sinkholes are systematic fractures in the bedrock. Three major types of joints occur in the Middle Mississippian rocks, which are approximately 325 to 355 million years old, of southern Indiana: vertical joints, inclined joints, and joints at right angles to cross-stratified rock beds. Vertical joints and often inclined joints have a tendency to form rectangular blocks of bedrock bounded by east-west-trending master joints and north-south-trending cross joints. Master joints commonly pass through multiple rock units, or beds, separated by bedding planes, while cross joints are limited to a single rock unit or bed of rock (Powell 1976). Cross joints commonly terminate at master joints and most always approach master joints at nearly right angles (fig. 3).

While caves usually form in limestone and dolomite, other natural materials determine how the cave will develop underground. Well-cemented shale and zones of chert interrupt the path of groundwater, often diverting and sustaining it above the local base level that groundwater is seeking (Powell 1976). Even the sediments transported by underground streams can affect changes in the routes of water. Cave passages that become filled

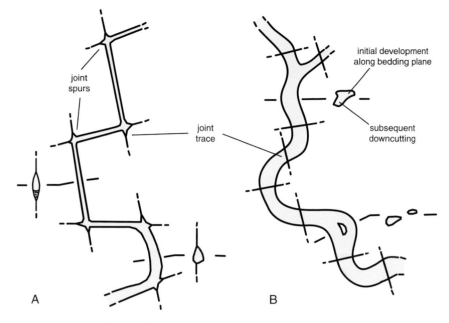

Figure 3. Plan-view diagram of (A) joint-oriented cave passage, and (B) a meandering cave passage. Both develop along joints, but low stream gradient results in the sinuous meanders. FROM POWELL (1976).

by fine-grained sediments (sand, silt, and clay) can force new stream routes to develop that circumvent the impediment that was deposited. Rock breakdown, created by the collapse of cave walls or ceilings, may also divert cave streams, causing them to create new passageways or enlarge existing passageways.

Cave Deposits and Cave Minerals

Cave deposits consist of soil deposits on the floor of a cave passage and dripstone or flowstone deposits on the floor, walls, or ceiling of a cave passage; the latter are generally termed *speleothems* (plate 2). Speleothems are called *secondary deposits* because they are created from materials derived by the dissolution of the overlying bedrock (Palmer 2007). Although many different minerals have been identified in cave deposits, most can be grouped into one of two families—calcium carbonate (calcite or aragonite) or hydrous calcium sulfate (gypsum).

Groundwater seeping downward through fissures and along joints in the bedrock dissolves calcium and bicarbonate ions. A molecule of calcium carbonate is deposited by escape of carbon dioxide, which is caused by a lowering of the carbon dioxide gas partial pressure or change in temperature at the point where the descending water comes into contact with the cave passage. Molecular attraction results in the growth of either an aragonite or calcite crystal (Hill and Forti 1997). The very high relative humidity and very low rate of evaporation in places where speleothems occur is strong evidence that evaporation is not significant to the stalactite-forming process.

The most common speleothems are stalactites (plate 2), which hang downward from the ceiling of the cave, and stalagmites, which are built upward from the floor. Stalactites often begin as hollow thin-walled tubes resembling drinking straws. As these increase in length, the central tube may become plugged, and water leakage at the upper terminus of the tube often allows deposits to build on the outside of the tube (Hill and Forti 1997).

Water that drops from stalactites can result in the deposition of mounds of calcium carbonate on the floor or a ledge; these mounds eventually become stalagmites. Stalactites and stalagmites can grow together to form columns of many sizes

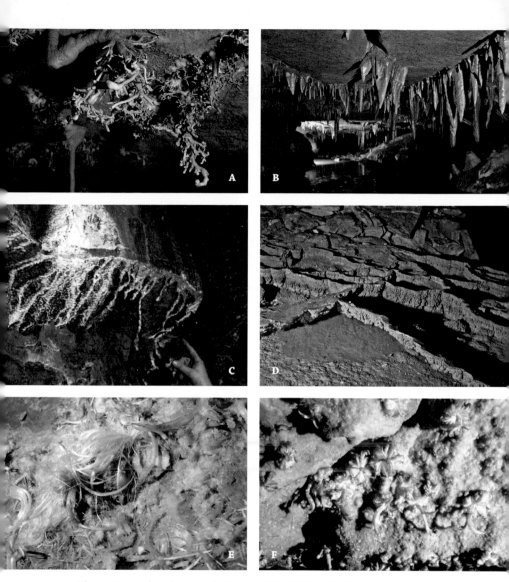

Plate 2. Examples of cave speleothems: (A) helictites; (B) stalactites; (C) moon milk; (D) rimstone dams; (E) epsomite crystals; and (F) gypsum flowers. PHOTOS BY SAMUEL S. FRUSHOUR AND RICHARD L. POWELL.

and shapes. Where stalactites grow broad and join together, they form what are called *draperies* on a wall or ledge. Sheets of water flowing or seeping over a surface can deposit a layer of flowstone. Temporary pools of slowly moving water sometimes build up rimstone dams around their edges as a result of aeration of the water where the velocity is greatest. Rimstone dams can also extend across cave streams where they range in thickness from approximately ¹⁄₁₆ of an inch to more than a foot and grow to several feet in height. During dry periods, evaporation of water, or anytime there is a loss of carbon dioxide from pools, results in floating thin plates—calcite or aragonite rafts. If a pool entirely dries up, the rafts become layers of corn flake–like chips on the bottom of the former pool.

Cave coral, helictites (plate 2), and anthodites are other varieties of calcium carbonate deposits occurring in caves. Their origin is not well understood, although we can gain some insight by reviewing their surroundings and form. Cave coral is botryoidal in shape and resembles clusters of tiny grapes or popped corn; these concretions are found on walls or floors. Their origin is attributed to precipitation of calcite at the air-rock-water interface or beneath the surface of temporary pools or pools with frequently changing water levels. The former water level of a pool is sometimes evident by the absence of cave coral above its former water surface.

Helictites are perhaps the most grotesque and often the most beautiful of all speleothems. They begin with a central canal much like a soda straw stalactite, but then twist, turn, and branch in many directions, seemingly at random. Their erratic growth is most likely caused by offsets in the joining of one calcite or aragonite crystal and the adjacent one, probably owing to changes in the route of capillary water traveling within the speleothem (Hill and Forti 1997). Helictites grow not only on ceilings but also may grow sideways from a wall or upward from a shelf or floor. They are uncommon in Indiana, but are found in profusion in a few caves.

Anthodites are straight, bladelike crystals of aragonite and are very rare in Indiana. They usually occur in clusters that radiate out from a single point of attachment on a cave wall or ceiling.

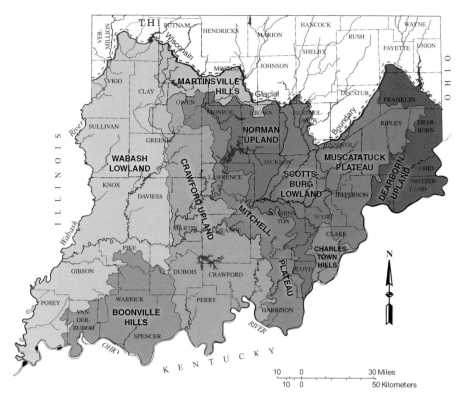

Figure 4. Map of the physiographic regions in southern Indiana. The Crawford Upland, Mitchell Plateau, Norman Upland, and Muscatatuck Plateau contain caves and karst features. MODIFIED FROM GRAY (2001).

The rate of growth of stalactites and other dripstone deposits apparently is quite slow and subject to considerable variation. Even the range of variation is poorly known. Soda straw stalactites have been documented to have grown a ½ inch in 10 years in Buckner Cave in Monroe County, Indiana, but much slower in Wyandotte Cave in Crawford County, Indiana. Tour guides in commercial caves may give figures such as 1 inch per 100 years, but growth rates actually vary with the seasons and depend on how much precipitation percolates into any portion of the cave from year to year.

Moon milk, a white pasty substance (plate 2), is an odd deposit that may be modified from dripstone by the action of bacteria. Mineralogically, it is a hydrated carbonate-hydroxide of magnesium. Moon milk occurs in only a few wet caves in Indiana and only in small quantities.

Gypsum in the form of selenite crystals is fairly abundant in certain caves, especially the drier cave passages of the Crawford Upland (fig. 4). Gypsum "flowers" of selenite (plate 2) appear to be extruded from the cave wall, but actually the process involves crystallization of the gypsum at the air-bedrock interface where calcium sulfate is brought to the wall of the cave by capillary water in the bedrock. Bundles of selenite needles also occur buried in unconsolidated deposits where sulfates are transported by moisture. The crystals grow in cave fill displacing the soil that surrounds them.

Epsom salts, a heptahydrate of magnesium sulfate (plate 2), occurs as a downy or powdery efflorescence on cave walls, or on cave floors as small needles. Deposits of Epsom salts can be found in Wyandotte Cave in Crawford County.

CAVE CLIMATE

The interiors of most caves have a relatively constant temperature and a high relative humidity and are devoid of light, creating an atmosphere of total darkness. Cave temperature is approximately equivalent to the average annual surface temperature of the area in which the cave is located. In Indiana, the typical temperature ranges from 53° to 54°F (11.8° to 12.2°C) (Palmer 2007). Observations demonstrate, however, that air currents and streams entering the cave may profoundly modify actual temperatures.

In many Indiana caves, you may notice air movement. The natural air circulation in the cave causes wind to blow out from or pull into the cave entrance. Large caves can exhibit frequent changes in air direction or *breathing*. Air movement is most obvious at a small or restricted place in an extensive cave. These air movements are primarily based on the density and temperature differences between the surface air and the cave air, but atmospheric pressure changes and the number and elevation of entrances to the cave certainly are involved in air flow characteristics as well. Air blowing from a cave entrance high on a hillside is primarily a winter phenomenon. When much of the cave interior is lower in elevation than the entrance, a chimney effect occurs. Warm air from the cave rises as a plume containing condensed moisture. During the summer, the same entrance may have relatively warm air drawn into it and cooled by the surrounding rock as cooled air in the cave flows to a lower entrance.

Caves are usually very wet or at least damp. Streams flow through many caves and they provide moisture; however, the atmosphere in caves is always at a high relative humidity. The deep interior of most caves is very damp year round with the moisture level in the air nearing 100 percent relative humidity. Water that has percolated down through overlying soil and rock fractures and drips from the ceiling will vary in volume with the seasons and the amount of precipitation near the cave. This moisture is sufficient to keep the atmospheric humidity high; therefore, little or no evaporation occurs. The cave atmosphere near an entrance may be at its driest during winter because cold air is drawn in and warmed, resulting in the evaporation of moisture from cave surfaces. During the warmer seasons, the same entrance will be as humid and damp as the deeper parts of the cave.

The Cave Fauna of Indiana

Julian J. Lewis and Salisa L. Lewis

Although the earliest works on cave life in Indiana date to the early 1870s, the single largest early contribution to our knowledge of the state's cave fauna was the result of an expedition by State Geologist W. S. Blatchley. For five weeks in 1896, Blatchley drove a two-horse spring wagon through the south-central Indiana karst region, mapping and collecting specimens from 20 caves. His sampling established the foundation of our knowledge of Indiana's cave fauna. This was built on by Arthur M. Banta with his 1907 treatise on the fauna of Mayfield's Cave, in Monroe County. More than just an analysis of a single cave, Banta encapsulated essentially everything that was known about the cave fauna of Indiana. In 1928, the Frenchmen C. Bolivar and R. Jeannel visited Marengo and Donaldson Caves, discovering numerous new species of troglobites in these significant sites.

Many other individuals have contributed to our knowledge of Indiana's cave fauna, through the preparation of numerous theses, reports, and published papers. Most of these have concentrated on narrow areas of interest, for example, taxonomic revisions of genera, descriptions of new species, ecological studies of individual sites, or checklists of species of an area. Over the past 35 years, we have visited over 500 Indiana caves for the purpose of sampling to amass a comprehensive understanding of the fauna. With the exception of the Northern cavefish, all troglobites in Indiana are invertebrates.

Although many challenges exist in the preservation of Indiana's unique subterranean biodiversity, many great strides have been made. Much of what is now known about the cave fauna of Indiana is due to bioinventory projects sponsored by the Nature Conservancy, Indiana Department of Natural Resources, Hoosier National Forest, and U.S. Fish and Wildlife Service. The results of these projects allow data-driven decisions

Plate 3. Some creatures found in Indiana caves: (A) the Northern cave fish (*Amblyopsis spelaea*) is found only south of the East Fork White River; (B) a cave crayfish is blind and has no pigmentation for coloration; (C) a cave salamander can be found in wet or damp caves and may leave the cave in search of food; (D) the big brown bat is found in numerous caves; (E) a variety of spider that is found near cave entrances. PHOTOS BY SAMUEL S. FRUSHOUR AND RICHARD L. POWELL.

in conservation planning for the caves and karst. Tens of thousands of acres of karstlands have been acquired by these agencies containing hundreds of caves. Ecological studies such as the long-term monitoring of the federal endangered Indiana bat take the conservation effort to a higher level in attempting to actively protect species teetering on the brink. Currently a program is being instituted to reintroduce numbers of Allegheny woodrats (*Neotoma magister*) to bolster the viability of this animal in the state.

Plate 4. Other creatures found in caves: (A) wood rats are found predominantly near the Ohio River; (B) isopods can be found in cave streams; (C) crickets can be encountered hundreds of feet from the ground surface; (D) beetles burrow into mud banks; and (E) moths may be found near the entrances of caves. PHOTOS BY JULIAN J. LEWIS AND SALISA L. LEWIS.

A significant obligate subterranean fauna (troglobites) exists in Indiana's caves, but the average observer is unlikely to see much of it without careful observation, as the animals are frequently tiny (less than 5 millimeters), confined to specific microhabitats, limited in their overall distribution to just a few caves, and sometimes seasonal in occurrence. That notwithstanding, some animals will be seen in almost any cave in Indiana. The following is an overview of the cave fauna of Indiana (plates 3 and 4).

Mammals. Four species of bats are the most commonly seen mammals. The smallest, the Eastern pipistrelle (*Perimyotis pipistrellus*) is ubiquitous, usually roosting individually. The endangered Indiana bat (*Myotis sodalis*) hibernates in large clusters in sites like Wyandotte Cave, but with the exception of "bachelor colonies" of males is absent from caves during the summer. The little brown bat (*Myotis lucifugus*) and big brown bat (*Eptesicus fuscus*) usually hang singly or in small clusters.

The white-footed mouse is perhaps the most common mammal in Indiana caves, but is rarely seen. Likewise, raccoons are common in our caves, although the latrines are seen much more frequently than the animals. The Allegheny woodrat is present in a few caves along the Ohio River in Harrison and Crawford Counties.

Birds. The Eastern phoebe (*Sayornis phoebe*) is commonly found in cave entrances, where it places its nest on the wall in the twilight zone.

Salamanders. The most brightly colored animals occurring in Indiana caves are undoubtedly the cave (*Eurycea lucifuga*) and long-tail salamanders (*E. longicauda*), which are bright orange and yellow, respectively, dotted with black spots or bars. The slimy salamander (*Plethodon glutinosus*) is solid black with white spots, while the related zigzag salamander (*P. dorsalis*) is shorter and mottled in appearance with a zigzag stripe down the back.

Fish. The only troglobitic vertebrate in Indiana is the Northern cavefish (*Amblyopsis spelaea*), which is known from numerous caves south of the East Fork White River. It occurs only in the south-central karst region, where it is usually found in places where there is relatively deep water. The banded sculpin (*Cottus carolinae*) is a bizarre-looking fish with a large head and mottled appearance that blends in remarkably well with the stream gravels it rests upon. It is a common fish in Indiana caves and sometimes occurs by the hundreds.

Crayfish. Two subspecies of the cave crayfish occur in Indiana, *Orconectes inermis inermis* from the Ohio River to about Monroe County, and *Orconectes inermis testii* in Monroe and Owen Counties. It occurs only in the south-central karst region. The troglophile *Cambarus laevis* occurs in both of Indiana's karst areas, and its paleness and relatively small eyes can lead to it being mistaken for its eyeless relative.

Isopods. The cave isopod *Caecidotea stygia* is ubiquitous in the caves of the south-central karst, and Clark and Jefferson Counties in southeastern Indiana. There it is replaced by the related *Caecidotea rotunda* in Jennings, Ripley, and Decatur Counties. The two species look essentially identical. The familiar pillbugs that roll into balls are also isopods, and almost all of them have been introduced from Europe. The native land isopods are tiny and not commonly seen.

Amphipods. The common amphipods in Indiana caves are in the genus *Crangonyx*. Packard's groundwater amphipod (*C. packardi*) is found in both karst areas. Barr's (*C. barri*) and the Indiana (*C. indianensis*) cave amphipods occur in the south-central karst region, while Lewis's cave amphipod (*C. lewisi*) is limited to the south-eastern karst region. Several undescribed species of *Stygobromus* are tiny and extremely rare, mostly found in drip water where they fall from their native habitats in the epikarst.

Millipedes. Several species of *Pseudotremia* are found in caves of the counties along the Ohio River, but most are very rare. They are typically about ¾ inch in length and vary from white to bluish, all with reduced eyes. The three more common species are the Indiana cave millipede (*P. indianae*) in the Blue

River basin, Salisa's cave millipede (*P. salisae*) from the Little Blue River, and the Clark cave millipede (*P. nefanda*) in Clark County. Sollman's cave millipede (*Scoterpes sollmani*) is completely white and eyeless. It is known only from two caves in Harrison and Crawford Counties. In the northern half of the south-central karst region, the straw-colored Bollman's cave millipede (*Conotyla bollmani*) is common.

Spiders. The most obvious spider in Indiana is the cave orb-weaver (*Meta ovalis*), first described from the Marengo Cave System. This large troglophile spins its prominent orb webs from cave walls, sometimes in association with its egg sacs. Several species of troglobitic spiders occur in Indiana, but most are tiny (in the neighborhood of 2 mm) sheet-web spiders. The subterranean sheet-web spider (*Phanetta subterranea*) probably occurs in nearly every cave in Indiana, where it is found under flat stones or sticks. Its web consists of a few fine threads in a fissure or between stones. The egg sacs are seen more frequently than the spiders, where the spiders stick them to the undersides of stones. Two other rarer cave spiders are known from Indiana (*Porrhomma cavernicola, Islandiana cavicola*), along with new species of another sheet-web spider as well as a leptonetid cave spider.

Pseudoscorpions. These animals resemble tiny scorpions without the stinger tails. Two general types are found in Indiana caves. The first (*Hesperochernes mirabilis*) is relatively common in mammal dens in caves, but has never been found in a surface habitat. It is brown with relatively short appendages. The other kind includes the unpigmented species that are either eyeless or have reduced eyes and possess elongate appendages. Examples of these range from the troglobitic Packard's cave pseudoscorpion (*Kleptochthonius packardi*), to the somewhat less troglomorphic Indiana cave pseudoscorpion (*Apochthonius indianensis*) to the troglophilic Lewis cave pseudoscorpion (*Kleptochtonius lewisorum*). Several new species are known from Indiana caves and await description.

Mites. Free-living mites are common in leaf litter and the cave mites (*Rhagidia s. latu*) are sometimes mistaken for small, confused spiders owing to their habit of rapidly running about mud banks in figure-8 patterns. Several kinds of mites, chiggers, and ticks are common on bats, woodrats, and raccoons.

Springtails. These tiny (usually a millimeter or less) insectlike creatures have an elongate structure on their underside that is similar to a loaded catapult. When the springtail is threatened, it uses this to leap into the air, sometimes several inches, which is many times the body length of the animal. Thus the name "spring tail." The micro-arthropods frequently constitute about a quarter of the troglobitic community in Indiana caves. Two forms are typical, the elongate species such as the cavernous springtail (*Sinella cavernarum*) or Indiana cave springtail (*Sinella alata*), or the globose forms such as Lewis's cave springtail (*Arrhopalites lewisi*). Dozens of other springtail species are recorded from Indiana caves.

Diplurans. These insects resemble white silverfish. They are very rare in Indiana caves and all of the known kinds remain as undescribed species (*Litocampa* spp.) new to science.

Crickets. Three species of cave crickets are common, but none are obligate cave animals and many related species live in Indiana's forests and prairies. The most familiar is the Stygian cave cricket (*Ceuthophilus stygius*), which occurs across the southern part of both of our karst areas as well as Kentucky and Tennessee. The Southern cave cricket (*C. meridionalis*) occurs with the Stygian, from which it can be easily separated by the prominent yellow stripe down its back. Hanging in clusters on the cave ceiling, these two crickets literally rub elbows. The spotted cave cricket (*C. brevipes*) is usually found around entrances, although it is more common in the northern part of the south-central karst area.

Beetles. Although many kinds of these insects occur in our caves, the ground beetles are the predominant group. The most commonly seen ground beetle in Indiana caves (*Platynus* *tenuicollis*) has large eyes, is dark brown with tan-colored legs, and is a widespread troglophile in the eastern United States. The much smaller troglobitic cave beetles (*Pseudanophthalmus*) are much smaller, mostly a ¼ inch or less in length. All are eyeless and unpigmented, which in cave beetles translates to red in color. Over a dozen kinds are known in Indiana, and many are incredibly rare, some remaining undescribed. The most commonly seen are the Wyandotte Cave beetle (*P. tenuis*) in Crawford, Harrison, and southern Washington Counties; the Marengo cave beetle (*P. stricticollis*) in northern Crawford and Washington, Orange, and Lawrence Counties; and the Shiloh cave beetle (*P. shilohensis*) in Lawrence, Monroe, and Owen Counties.

The rove beetles are probably the most common beetles in Indiana caves. The largest, the Spelean rove beetle (*Quedius spelaeus*), is mostly red in color and about ½ inch in length. It is widespread in the United States, where it is usually found on various sorts of animal droppings (common in raccoon latrines). Over a dozen other rove beetle species are commonly found in our caves, although all are inconspicuous in color and small in size, less than a ¼ inch in length.

The rarest animals in this group in the state are the ant beetles. Krekeler's cave beetle (*Batrisodes krekeleri*) is known from four caves in Clark, Crawford, and Lawrence Counties. An undescribed cave ant beetle is known from one cave in the Hoosier National Forest in Monroe County (*Batriasymmodes*). Other beetles that are sometimes found in Indiana caves are feather-winged beetles, round fungus beetles, scarab beetles, and carrion beetles.

Flies. The first animal a visitor is likely to see in an Indiana cave is a fly, hanging on the ceiling near the entrance. Two species are common (*Culex pipiens, Anopheles punctipennis*). One kind of fly is troglobitic, the cave dung fly (*Spelobia tenebrarum*). This small black fly is commonly found on animal droppings and comes to cheese bait in almost any cave habitat. A troglophile, the cave hump-backed fly (*Megaselia cavernicola*) is equally common. The pinkish-brown heleomyzid flies (*Aecothea specus, Amoebaleria defessa*) are easily seen on cave walls. Other common kinds in Indiana caves are the fungus gnats (so-called glow-worms) and moth flies.

Moths. One kind commonly overwinters and is frequently noticed owing to its rather bright pink coloration. The herald moth (*Scoliopteryx libatrix*) is the harbinger of winter in Indiana caves.

Snails. Both aquatic and land snails live in Indiana caves. The troglobitic Spiral cave snail (*Antroselates spiralis*) occurs only in cave streams in the Blue River basin. Many calcium-loving land snails live around the entrances to caves, such as the attractively banded alternate anguispira (*Anguispira alternata*), or common three-toothed snail (*Triodopsis tridentata*) with the three "teeth" in the shell's opening. The inflected land snail (*Inflectarius inflectus*) lives deeper in caves and may be a troglophile.

Flatworms. One kind occurs in caves across both karst belts, Weingartner's cave flatworm (*Sphalloplana weingartneri*). These small worms are free-living (not parasites) and are almost always found on the undersides of stones. In quiet pools, they may glide upside down on the surface tension of the water.

The majority of Indiana caves are located in Mississippian bedrock that is part of the physiographic region of south-central Indiana. The Mitchell Plateau (fig. 4) is underlain predominantly by limestone. Bedrock of the Mitchell Plateau dips to the southwest at a rate of about 25 feet per mile (fig. 5) and the region has a total thickness of more than 450 feet of rocks of the West Baden and Blue River Groups in the south-central part of the state. The Crawford Upland, to the west of the Mitchell Plateau

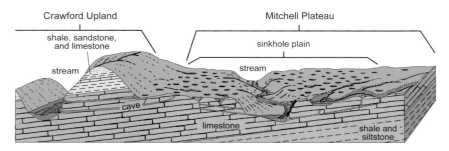

Figure 5. Idealized cross-section of the Crawford Upland and Mitchell Plateau. HASENMUELLER AND POWELL (2005).

Figure 6. (OPPOSITE) Generalized stratigraphic column of Mississippian bedrock in south-central Indiana. MODIFIED FROM THOMPSON AND SOWDER (2006). These rocks are younger and underlie the Mansfield Formation of the Pennsylvanian period. Caves occur predominantly in rocks of the Stephensport, West Baden, Blue River, and Sanders Groups. Brackets indicate bedrock where caves may be found. BEDROCK THICKNESSES ARE FROM SHAVER ET AL. (1986).

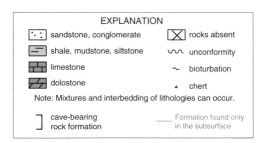

PERIOD	APPROX. THICKNESS (feet)	LITHOLOGY	ROCK UNIT		
			SIGNIFICANT MEMBER	FORMATION	GROUP
M I S S I S S I P P I A N	30 to 300		— Negli Creek Ls. — Leopold Ls.	Grove Church Sh. Kinkaid Ls.	south-central
				Degonia Fm.	Tobinsport Fm.
				Clore Fm.	
				Palestine Fm.	
				Menard Ls.	Branchville Fm.
				Waltersburg Fm.	
				Vienna Ls.	
				Tar Springs Fm.	
	120 to 200			Glen Dean Ls.	Stephens-port
				Hardinsburg Fm.	
				Haney Ls.	
				Big Clifty Fm.	
				Beech Creek Ls.	
	100 to 250			Cypress Fm. / Elwren Fm.	West Baden
				Reelsville Ls.	
				Sample Fm.	
				Beaver Bend Ls.	
				Bethel Fm.	
	250 to 650			Paoli Ls.	Blue River
				Ste. Genevieve Ls.	
				St. Louis Ls.	
	125 to 800			Salem Ls.	Sanders
				Harrodsburg Ls.	
				Muldraugh Fm. / Ramp Creek Fm.	
	3 to 750		— Floyds Knob Ls.	Edwardsville Fm.	Borden
				Spickert Knob Fm.	
				New Providence Sh.	

| | | | | | Buffalo Wallow |

(fig. 4), is underlain by limestone, shale, and sandstone strata that also dip to the southwest. Because of the sloping bedrock, the surficial rocks become younger from east to west in the Mitchell Plateau and Crawford Upland.

The principal cave-bearing rocks of southeastern Indiana are limestone, dolomite, and shale of Silurian and Devonian age located in the Muscatatuck Plateau (fig. 4). There are some glacially buried karst features in Ordovician rocks as well. The bedrock dip to the southwest is slightly less than in the south-central cave and karst region and rock formations are generally thinner. Mississippian (fig. 6), Devonian, and Silurian cave-bearing, or cave-associated, rocks are described in appendix I.

Karst Features

Karst features are landforms characteristic of areas underlain by limestone or other soluble rock. Karst features form where soil water or groundwater has dissolved the soluble bedrock of an area, although dissolution of bedrock may occur without the development of ground-surface karst features. The most easily recognized karst features are the various forms of sinkholes. Other karst features are swallow holes, blind valleys, karst valleys, caves, grikes, lapiés, and springs (Powell 1961). Sometimes springs occur within spring alcoves or steep heads. Some sinkholes and springs are also cave entrances. All of these karst features indicate the presence of underground drainage routes through solution-enlarged joints, fractures, and caves.

Traditionally, the term *karst* is used to define a terrain having the features previously mentioned. But the definition of karst is evolving. Some researchers have included certain features found underground, including joints, fractures, solution-enlarged conduits, and caves, in their definition of karst. The expanded definition of karst may be acceptable for modern researchers; however, the term *karst* is most correctly used as a terrain, or surface feature, expression of bedrock dissolution.

The term *karst* also is often used incorrectly in popular literature when referring to bedrock and groundwater. Bedrock is not karst and neither is groundwater.

Sinkholes

Surface runoff into sinkholes or intermittent streams that terminate in swallow holes is common to karst areas drained via bedrock aquifers. Sinkholes are the most observed karst feature and the one most associated with karst areas. They are depressions on the surface of the ground that result from dissolution and mechanical weathering of near-surface bedrock, downward

A. Sapping

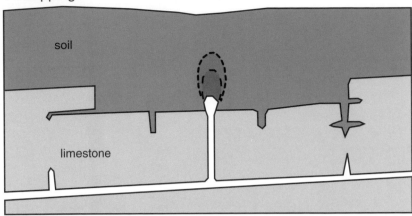

B. Collapse

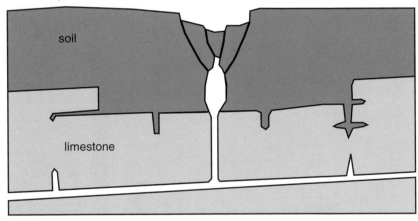

C. Erosion

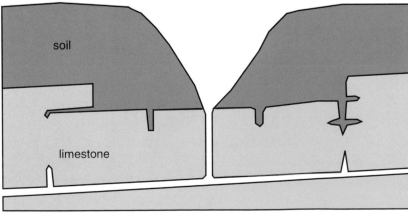

Figure 8. A sinkhole exhibiting soil subsidence.
PHOTO BY SAMUEL S. FRUSHOUR.

sapping or piping of soil, collapse of soil into fractures or voids (fig. 7), or collapse of bedrock into a void or cave. Any of these processes may result in a depression feature called a sinkhole. Many sinkholes begin as a small depression or hole that may be only a few inches across, but it has the potential to grow and sometimes extend to cover dozens of acres. Some sinkholes enlarge and coalesce or form compound sinkholes. The initial surface expression of a sinkhole may form rapidly by overnight collapse of a soil bridge or thin bedrock (fig. 8) over a void. The precursor or warning of possible sinkhole formation may be a sag in the ground surface or a hole that looks like an animal burrow and is called a *soil pipe*. A soil pipe is a small tunnel where water carries soil downward to a subsurface cavity. Once a small sinkhole is formed, erosion on the ground surface and

Figure 7. (LEFT) Schematic drawing of progressive development of a sinkhole by (A) soil sapping, (B) soil collapse, and (C) slope retreat owing to erosion and subsidence. DRAWING BY R. L. POWELL.

Figure 9. A sinkhole formed as a result of collapse of bedrock.
PHOTO BY SAMUEL S. FRUSHOUR.

additional underground soil collapse, soil sapping, and slumping promote its enlargement. The steepness of the sides of a
sinkhole depends on its age, on whether plant root systems hold
the soil, and on whether agricultural use of the land caused extensive soil erosion that leads to gentler soil slopes.

A collapse sinkhole resulting from the actual falling of rock
into a cave below it is uncommon. Most sinkholes are the result

of soil moving underground along solution-enlarged joints or fractures in the bedrock. The entrance of Bluespring Caverns and Fuzzy Hole in the Hoosier National Forest (fig. 9) are two examples of collapse sinkholes that formed when the bedrock below the bottom of an existing sinkhole collapsed into a cave.

When collapse of a cave roof exposes horizontal passage-ways that can be accessed in two directions, it is called a *karst window*. The two entrances at Bronson Cave and the Twin Caves entrances in Spring Mill State Park each had a segment of cave passage that collapsed, creating cave entrances separated by a karst window. When a large collapse sinkhole has steep rocky walls and a relatively flat alluvial floor, perhaps with a stream rising and sinking within it, it is called a *gulf*. Wesley Chapel Gulf, located between Orangeville and Indiana Highway 37, covers more than 6 acres and has within it a large spring and several swallow holes.

Some of the numerous sinkholes in the Mitchell Plateau become plugged and hold water, although many drain because of soil subsidence. Between Livonia and Campbellsburg, where the underground drainage routes are small and close to the ground surface, some broad but very shallow depressions have developed that do not drain well. These are sinkhole swamps, karst swamps, or fens. These appear as isolated sinkholes containing lush plants and soggy soil.

Swallow Holes

Swallow holes, or swallets, are holes where flowing water goes underground. They may be located in blind valleys, sinkholes, or stream beds (fig. 10). Many of the small streams of the Mitchell Plateau and in the Crawford Upland are sinking streams that disappear into swallow holes. Numerous dry stream beds and sinkholes near the base of ridges in the Crawford Upland have swallow holes that only take water during the wet season or during heavy rains. The Lost River region of Orange County has some dramatic examples where sinking streams draining

Figure 10. A dry bed and swallow hole. Runoff of storm waters collects in dry beds during rain events and sinks into swallow holes. PHOTO BY SAMUEL S. FRUSHOUR.

several square miles are swallowed by individual swallets or groups of swallow holes (Malott 1952).

BLIND VALLEYS

Blind valleys exist where piracy of surface drainage into swallow holes has occurred to such an extent that all surface flow goes entirely underground (fig. 11). Surface water no longer flows beyond a saddlelike ridge at the downstream terminus of the valley. At the junction of Airport Road and Indiana Highway 45 near Bloomington is a group of swallow holes at the southern end of a mile-long blind valley.

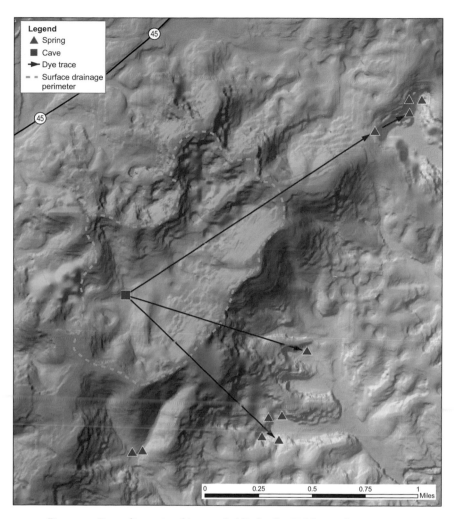

Figure 11. Three-dimensional image of a blind valley in Monroe County. There is no stream bed on the ground surface and subsurface dye traces, shown by arrows, indicate that water flow is to three springs.

Karst Valleys

Similar to the blind valley is the karst valley, which may contain a variety of karst features. The floors of karst valleys in the Crawford Upland may have sinkholes, swallow holes, and the occasional spring (fig. 12). Karst valleys are developed much

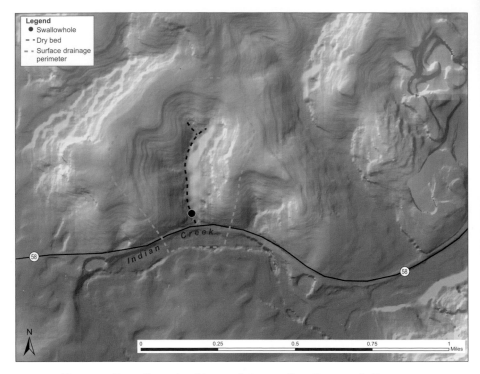

Figure 12. Three-dimensional image of a karst valley adjacent to Indian Creek in Lawrence County. Although water sinks into the valley floor, excess floodwater flows on the ground surface to the nearby creek.

like the blind valley, by surface erosion downcutting through nonsoluble strata such as shale and sandstone downward into limestone. Floodwaters can find their way out of the valley on the ground surface, unlike the blind valley. The valley floors sometimes have small sinkhole plains elevated above the level of nearby permanent surface streams. A prominent feature of karst valleys in the Crawford Upland is the dry stream bed, or dry bed, that is normally a dry, rocky streambed containing water only during periods of heavy precipitation (fig. 13).

SPRINGS

Springs are important karst features because they exist where groundwater surfaces or emerges after moving through

Figure 13. Dry stream beds are indicators of subsurface drainage and are a significant karst feature. PHOTO BY SAMUEL S. FRUSHOUR.

subsurface conduit systems and caves (fig. 14). They are the ultimate discharge point for water draining into karst features and infiltrating subsurface drainage systems to flow through solution conduits and caves. The amount of water flowing from a spring reflects the size of its watershed, or drainage area, and the amount of precipitation. Springs that issue water from soluble bedrock and flow perennially (year-round), are found in each of the Indiana karst areas. In the southeastern karst region, springs are found exclusively along stream valleys, as are most caves. Some of these springs discharge subterranean water flow from both bedrock conduits and overlying glacially deposited sediments.

Figure 14. A spring in the Crawford Upland situated near the valley floor.
PHOTO BY SAMUEL S. FRUSHOUR.

In the Mitchell Plateau and adjacent parts of the Crawford Upland, springs are usually found along the major streams and in the walls of some sinkholes. Some springs of the Mitchell Plateau are located in valleys that eventually join major streams. The springs or spring caves of Cave River Valley and Spring Mill State Park are in valleys that ultimately join with the major stream of the entire region—the East Fork White River.

The numerous springs in the Crawford Upland are associated with the thin limestones of the West Baden and Stephensport Groups. Water issues from the Beech Creek Limestone and Glen Dean Limestone (fig. 6). Small springs, or seeps, in the Crawford Upland are usually in the head of valleys that intrude into the flanks of ridges. Larger springs or spring caves (fig. 15) are often down valley adjacent to surface streams or are the origin of surface streams. Springs usually discharge groundwater that traveled under the flanks of ridges or entire karst valleys.

Figure 15. Old Town Spring Cave entrance in Crawford County.
PHOTO BY SAMUEL S. FRUSHOUR.

Where springs occur at the base of hillsides, the rock surrounding them may weather and crumble, causing the spring
outlet to recede and form a spring alcove. Given enough time
for rock above a spring to weather, a steep head may form at
the head of a valley or alcove with its slope angle steeper than
adjoining slopes. Greene County has a number of well-formed
steep heads with water issuing from the Beech Creek Limestone.

CAVE ENTRANCES

Cave entrances are coincidental in origin to the formation of
the cave. There are likely many caves in Indiana that do not have
entrances that are accessible by humans. Most cave passages
develop nearly horizontally, while some are vertical. Whether
or not caves have entrances large enough to allow human egress
depends on various geologic processes. Most cave entrances are
openings in sinkholes or are spring outlets. The downcutting of

Figure 16. Pit or vertical shaft in Monroe County. PHOTO BY ELLIOT STAHL.

valleys may intersect or truncate a cave passageway to create an entrance on a hillside.

Some entrances on hillsides are atop fallen rock where the cave ceiling has progressively collapsed upward, perhaps with a spring issuing from the base of the rubble. Many cave entrances are in sinkholes, owing to the sinkhole-forming processes of soil sapping or piping and soil collapse into sinkholes and into cavities in the bedrock. Pits or vertical shafts (fig. 16) that are

Figure 17. A swallow hole cave entrance in Greene County.
PHOTO BY SAMUEL S. FRUSHOUR.

open to the air have entrances and occur mostly in the Crawford Upland in Indiana. Pits may have sinkhole or rock outcrop
entrances and are often found where water from sandstone or
perched on shale finds its way down into the underlying limestone. Sinkholes over cave passages can become cave entrances
through subsidence of soil or rock collapse and some swallow
holes (fig. 17) are cave entrances where the swallow hole is not
obstructed by collapsed rock, mud, or forest debris.

Figure 18. Solution-enlarged joints and fractures in the
Ste. Genevieve Limestone in a road cut in Lawrence County.
PHOTO BY SAMUEL S. FRUSHOUR.

EPIKARST

Solution features, such as solution-enlarged joints and exposed
lapiés that are part of the bedrock surface and fractures within
the upper part of the bedrock and that have been aggressively
enlarged by solution are called *epikarst* (Klimchouk et al. 2000).
The epikarst zone may be only a few feet depending on the
amount of solution along the fractures, which in turn depends
upon the thickness and type of lithology at or near the rock
surface (fig. 18). Large amounts of groundwater may be stored
in the epikarst zone. The acidic water in the epikarst zone is
most aggressive where the overlying soil is abundant in organic
detritus; however, contact with limestone quickly reduces the
acidic nature of the downward-migrating water.

GARRISON CHAPEL VALLEY

As surface streams eroded through various lithologies of the West Baden Group (fig. 6) in the eastern part of the Crawford Upland, they eventually cut into limestone of the Blue River Group (Powell 1970). Once limestone of the Blue River Group became exposed, the surface water was diverted into joints and fractures in the limestone to become groundwater in a process called *subterranean stream piracy*. The groundwater then moved down vertically and horizontally through the joints that gradually enlarged, carrying progressively more water from adjoining tributary fractures. When swallow holes along the course of a stream are able to take the entire volume of runoff water, the stream channel becomes a dry bed carrying only storm water. This process is common in the Mississippian limestone of the Crawford Upland. An example lies 7 miles southwest of Bloomington where Garrison Chapel Road winds through a sinkhole-floored karst valley (fig. 19).

Traveling west on Airport Road from Indiana Highway 45 in Monroe County, one ascends a ridge that is the Springville Escarpment; however, the road soon descends a few feet into the part of the karst valley where sinkholes are numerous and occasional swallow holes are found. The head of the karst valley (Wayne 1949), where stream downcutting has led to subterranean stream piracy and developed a large cave system, is 4,000 feet north of Airport Road. The Maderis-Salamander-Turtle-Shaft-Grotto Cave System transmits water sinking in the valley head and from an adjacent valley in the northeast. This groundwater travels west to a spring in Coon Hollow and eventually to Richland Creek.

The valley abruptly deepens 1,000 feet southwest of the junction of Airport Road and Garrison Chapel Road, where intensive drainage into the subsurface was formed with water

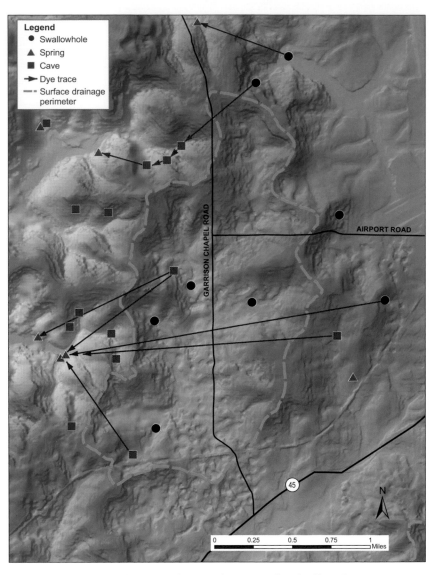

Figure 19. Three-dimensional image of Garrison Chapel Valley, a karst valley in Monroe County, showing the topography, valley perimeter, cave openings, springs, swallow holes, and subsurface dye traces.

transmitted westward through Wayne Cave to springs in Blair Hollow. The valley widens to nearly ½ mile south of the Wayne Cave source area and has many broad sinkholes that have been partly filled in by erosion from poor farming practices. This is the principal source area for water in the extensive Buckner Cave and Queen Blair Cave. Groundwater in these two caves emerges at Blair Springs in Blair Hollow.

The smaller Blair Spring is fed by groundwater that originates as precipitation in the south part of the blind valley and flows through the Blair Cave System. The direction of water travel is to the northwest, unlike the west-southwest pattern of drainage routes elsewhere under the valley and adjoining ridges.

The Blair Hollow springs discharge water that falls as precipitation in the karst valley and on the flanks of the adjacent ridges that contain cave systems. Concurrent with development of karst drainage in the valley floor, infiltration of precipitation into sandstone of the Elwren and Sample Formations on the flanks of developing ridges was forming drainage networks and caves in the underlying Paoli and Ste. Genevieve Limestones. Subsurface stream tracing using dyes has shown that the drainage in three large caves east of the blind valley have streams that pass under the floor of the valley and emerge at Blair Springs.

American Bottoms Valley

The American Bottoms region is the site of a former glacial lake of pre-Wisconsin, or Illinoian age, in eastern Greene County in the present valley of Bridge Creek. It is located south of State Highway 54 and about 8 miles east of Bloomfield. The drainage area is approximately 10½ square miles, and the bottom of the valley is farmland with fertile soil that is unusual for this ridge and valley country (fig. 20).

As an eastward-facing glacial ice front was melting, extensive outwash of clastic material (clay, silt, sand, and gravel) once incorporated in the ice, flowed out in great aprons that

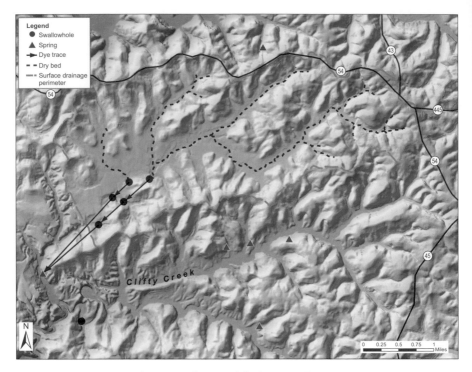

Figure 20. Three-dimensional image of the American Bottoms region blind valley in Greene County showing the valley perimeter with five major swallow holes and subsurface dye traces to Bennett Spring.

effectively blocked drainage of the valley of Bridge Creek, Beech Creek to the north, and Clifty Creek to the south. The latter two streams eventually reestablished their drainage westward while the water in the lake in the American Bottoms valley did not reestablish surface flow to the west. Instead, subsurface drainage developed in the Beech Creek Limestone that crops out on hillsides of a valley to the west and exists below the American Bottoms valley floor (Malott 1919). A series of five swallow holes developed to divert the drainage of Bridge Creek westward to Bennett Spring, which is located at the base of a bluff 1 mile southwest of the westernmost swallow hole. With development

Figure 21. Prominent features of the Lost River drainage area in Orange County. MODIFIED FROM POWELL (1961).

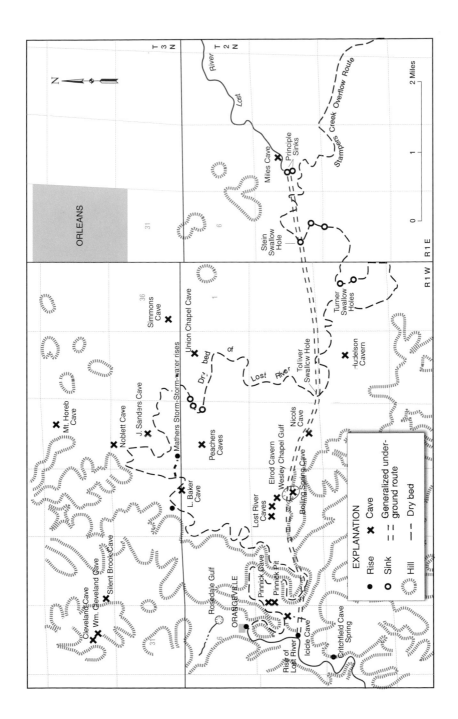

EXPLANATION

× Cave

● Rise   = = Generalized under-
                 ground route

○ Sink

      Hill   — — Dry bed

of subsurface drainage, the floor of the valley was not eroded to the elevation of nearby surface streams. The caves under the floor of the valley are entered via swallow holes. These caves are extremely flood-prone and quickly fill with stormwater.

LOST RIVER REGION

Nearly all the features of a karst terrain are present in the Lost River drainage area. The most common feature is a sinkhole; however, classic examples of swallow holes, dry beds or over-flow channels, blind valleys, karst valleys, sinkhole ponds, karst fens, karst windows, dolines, collapse sinkholes, gulfs, springs, cave springs, and alluviated cave springs are exemplified in the region as well (fig. 21). The region was made world famous by the pioneering efforts of Indiana University professor Clyde A. Malott, who published on his investigations during the first half of the twentieth century.

Lost River originates in Washington County, where it flows westward as a surface stream until it reaches the eastern margin of an area that has numerous sinkholes. There it sinks into the limestone bedrock and flows through solution conduits and caverns to reemerge 7 miles to the west. Downstream of the river's first swallow holes is about 22 miles of meandering dry bed that carries water only during wet periods. Lost River is the second largest sinking stream in the state, having over 48 square miles of drainage disappearing underground. The largest in the state is Indian Creek near Corydon in Harrison County. The entire Lost River drainage basin contains about 355 square miles within the Mitchell Plateau and the Crawford Upland physiographic units (fig. 4) (Rea 1992).

The Lost River Watershed can be divided into four parts determined in part on the basis of tracing the normal and low-flow

Figure 22. Dye traces are indicators of the general direction of groundwater flow in the Lost River area of karst features. Water that sinks in the region emerges at springs. MODIFIED FROM HASENMUELLER ET AL. (2003).

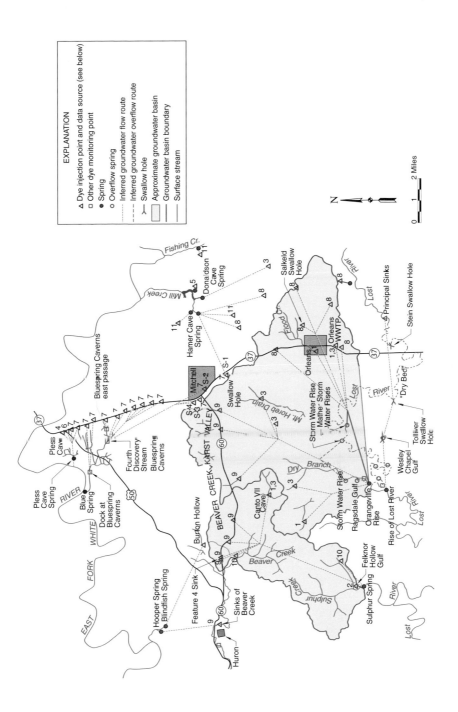

EXPLANATION

△ Dye injection point and data source (see below)
□ Other dye monitoring point
● Spring
○ Overflow spring
----- Inferred groundwater flow route
---- Inferred groundwater overflow route
⊁ Swallow hole
▨ Approximate groundwater basin
Groundwater basin boundary
— Surface stream

0 1 2 Miles

Figure 23. The Orangeville Rise, in Orange County, is a large spring where groundwater in the northern part of the Lost River drainage area emerges to form a surface stream. PHOTO BY SAMUEL S. FRUSHOUR.

subterranean drainage using subsurface dye tracing techniques (fig. 22). (1) The northeastern part includes 40$\frac{7}{10}$ square miles in the Crawford Upland and Mitchell Plateau that is tributary to the Orangeville Rise. (2) The central portion covers 108$\frac{4}{5}$ square miles of drainage within the Mitchell Plateau and partly within the Crawford Upland. This area includes the upper, or eastern, part of Lost River that is tributary to the Rise of Lost River. This portion includes most of the dry bed and sinkhole plain area commonly associated with Lost River. (3) The southern part is the karst valley of the South Fork of Stamper Creek that is a tributary to Lick Creek, an area of about 15 square miles. (4) The western part of the Lost River region consists of about 192 square miles of surface drainage area downstream of the Rise of Lost River.

Excess water within the entire drainage basin fills the subterranean conduits and overflows into surface flood channels
or dry beds. The water ultimately discharges into Lost River,
downstream of the Orangeville Rise, where the Lost River is a
permanent surface stream. Modern floods essentially reoccupy
the late Tertiary or early Pleistocene surface routes that were
regularly used prior to the development of karst features and
caverns during early and middle Pleistocene time (Powell 1964).

The features of Lost River that are most accessible are the
Principle Sinks and Stein Swallow Hole (both located on private
property), Wesley Chapel Gulf (in the Hoosier National Forest),
and the Orangeville Rise (fig. 23) (owned by the Indiana Karst
Conservancy, but publicly accessible).

The Principle Sinks of Lost River are a group of swallow holes
found in the stream bed by traveling three blocks from the
center of Orleans on Highway 337 and then south on a county
road about 3 miles to the normally dry bed of Lost River. The
Principle Sinks are ¼ mile east, upstream of the bridge. Water
disappears underground dramatically, as the size of the stream
is reduced when it passes each swallet. Some of the swallow
holes have small, noisy whirlpools and others are little more
than cracks in the bedrock with water cascading into them. The
first sink of Lost River is 1 mile farther upstream, but it is evident only during very low-flow conditions where some stream
flow sinks into the gravel, while the rest of the water continues
downstream in the surface channel. Floodwater that bypasses
the Principle Sinks flows to small swallets along the dry bed
and to Stein Swallow Hole (Rea 1992). Stein Swallow Hole consists of multiple swallets at the terminus of a dry bed located
⅓ mile east of State Highway 37 and ½ mile south of the road
to Orangeville. The area is alluviated but numerous swallow
holes have developed in the floor of two basins. Many swallow holes are obscured by masses of trees and tree limb debris
(timber rafts) that are left behind as floodwater recedes. As an
indicator of bedrock removal and of the uneven nature of the

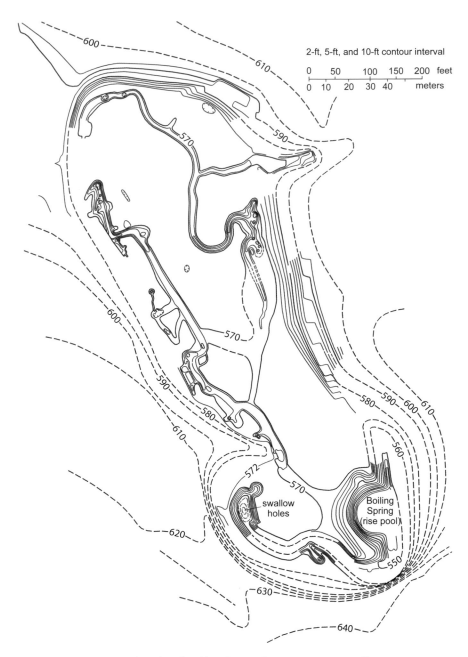

2-ft, 5-ft, and 10-ft contour interval

Figure 24. Wesley Chapel Gulf, in Orange County, is an 8-acre collapse
sinkhole where progressive collapse and sedimentation has partially
blocked the underground Lost River. The underground stream rises to the
surface but soon sinks again at a swallow hole. MAP BY RICHARD L. POWELL.

bedrock surface, there is a rock outcrop that partially encircles the larger of two basins.

Wesley Chapel Gulf is situated ½ mile south of Wesley Chapel and just south of the road to Orangeville. This is possibly the most striking feature of the Lost River area. The gulf is a large collapse sinkhole approximately 1,000 feet long and averaging 350 feet wide (fig. 24). The walls of the gulf range from 25 to 95 feet high and the relatively flat alluviated floor covers approximately 8 acres. Tertiary-age surface drainage was to the west prior to the collapse and probably resulted in the development of one or more swallow holes (Rea 1992). The gulf was likely formed by the collapse of a network of several cave passages where Elrod Cave to the north brought water from the east and joined cave passages that also brought water from the east and continued in a westerly direction.

Underground streams may develop wide, collapse-prone passageways at junctions where deposited sediments cause the natural lateral movement of streams. The consequence of this process was the creation of wide passageways and ceiling collapse to the ground surface. A result of collapse was an influx of surface water, collapse debris, and sediment from swallow holes in the overlying valley. Diversion conduits were forced to develop that circumvent the region of ongoing collapse and deposition of soil from the ground surface. The resulting gulf, bordered by cliffs, contains a spring rise and swallow holes. Boiling Spring emerges as a pool in the southeast part of the gulf (fig. 24). At normal water levels, the spring outflow travels only a few feet before sinking, but with increased flow, a dry bed channel carries floodwater across the floor of the gulf to a large swallow hole in the southwest part of the gulf. Stormwater flowing into the swallow hole then joins underground flow that circumvents the mass of rock and soil of the gulf floor (Rea 1992). Drainage west of the gulf travels westward through cave passages to the Rise of Lost River located about ¾ mile south of Orangeville.

KARST AND CAVE AREAS
OF INDIANA

Extending southward from Putnam County to the Ohio River is an internationally recognized area known for its abundance of karst features. A sequence of Mississippian limestones, sandstones, and shales occurs in this area which is not covered by the glacial drift that masks the bedrock over five-sixths of Indiana (fig. 4) (DesMarais et al. 1973). Owen and Putnam Counties were glaciated, burying some karst features. Karst features are more obvious in Crawford, Greene, Harrison, Lawrence, Monroe, Orange, and Washington Counties. A southeastern karst and cave region in Bartholomew, Clark, Decatur, Jefferson, Jennings, Ripley, and Switzerland Counties is developed in Silurian and Devonian carbonate rocks but is extensively covered by glacial till and outwash. Subsequent erosion uncovered some sinkholes and excavated glacially buried valleys exposing springs and caves. Small sections of Dearborn, Jefferson, Ohio, Ripley, and Switzerland Counties are karst areas in Ordovician limestone. In Delaware and Grant Counties of northern Indiana, buried karst and caves have been exposed by quarrying, and at least one glacially buried cave was exposed by erosion.

There are four physiographic regions in Indiana where karst features may be found—from east to west, the Muscatatuck Plateau, the Norman Upland, the Mitchell Plateau, and the Crawford Upland. In each of them, there are areas of surface karst features where no known enterable caves exist. On the other hand, caves have formed in areas lacking surface karst features except for the occasional spring or cave entrance. Outside the karst regions, Delaware, Grant, Tippecanoe, Vanderburgh, and Wabash Counties have one or more caves; Grant County has a large sinkhole and other extensive solution features and sediment-filled caves exposed in a quarry.

THE SOUTH-CENTRAL KARST AND CAVE AREA

The karst areas of south-central Indiana are developed on and within the Mississippian carbonate rocks that lie in physiographic regions known as the Norman Upland, the Mitchell Plateau (formerly Mitchell Plain), and the Crawford Upland (fig. 4). These regions are physiographic subunits of the Highland Rim of the east-central United States (DesMarais et al. 1973).

The majority of Indiana's karst features and caves are located in the Mitchell Plateau and in limestone ridges usually capped by sandstone in the Crawford Upland. These two physiographic regions are important karst areas owing to five factors. (1) The low regional dip of the bedrock, approximately 25 feet per mile to the south-southwest, has allowed dissolution of limestone over a large continuous area. (2) The limestone is not covered by glacial deposits. (3) The humid climate of southern Indiana is favorable for solution processes. (4) The limestones have well-defined bedding planes, are jointed, and are fractured. (5) Base-level streams are incised deeply into the limestone with the result that steep local hydraulic gradients favor karst and cave development (DesMarais et al. 1973).

The south-central karst area lies on the west flank of the northwest-southeast-trending Cincinnati Arch, an anticline structure, where the bedrock dips southwestward into the Illinois Basin, whose deepest part is located in southeastern Illinois (fig. 25). The southwestward dip of the rock strata is pervasive but small local structures vary from this in both the amount of dip and orientation. The major bedrock structural deformation of the area is along the north-south-trending Mt. Carmel Fault zone and the syncline and Leesville Anticline which run parallel to it on the west along the western margin of the Norman Upland. Cavern development in the Cave River Valley area of Washington County and to the east of Highway 446 in Lawrence County has been influenced by these folds in the bedrock.

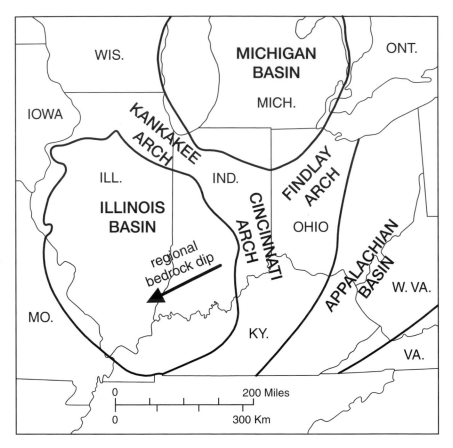

Figure 25. Map of the Midwest showing bedrock structural features. The arrow indicates the direction of the regional bedrock dip of southern Indiana. MODIFIED FROM HILL (2004).

The Knobstone Escarpment that faces eastward and its westward component, the Norman Upland, were formed by streams on siltstones, thick shale units, and thin limestone in the Borden Group of early Mississippian age. These rocks lie beneath the carbonate bedrock units of the Sanders and Blue River Groups of middle Mississippian age that thicken to the west to become the surface and substrata of the Mitchell Plateau with its characteristic karst topography. Only a few caves and sinkholes exist within the Norman Upland west of the Mt. Carmel Fault.

Figure 26. Oblique image and digital elevation model of the Crawford Upland, Mitchell Plateau, and East Fork White River valley. The river is the base-level stream of this region. MAP COURTESY OF DENVER HARPER, INDIANA GEOLOGICAL SURVEY.

The Mitchell Plateau is subdivided into distinct areas. To the south of the East Fork White River it is less dissected than to the north (fig. 26), and large areas, such as south of Spring Mill State Park, are characterized by hundreds of sinkholes to over 1,000 per mile square section of land in some areas (fig. 27) (Des-Marais et al. 1973). The sinkhole plain lies adjacent to deeply entrenched surface stream drainage and cavernous drainage such as is found at Cave River Valley and Spring Mill State Park. The eastern portion of the Mitchell Plateau in Washington County is characterized by surface drainage. Caves have developed to a lesser degree in this area. The eastern boundary of the Mitchell Plateau with the Norman Upland is transitional in Washington County and not well defined, but the transition of the surface drainage to the subsurface of the sinkhole plain is definable as

Figure 27. Aerial photograph of the landscape dominated by sinkholes of the Mitchell Plateau in the vicinity of Mitchell, Lawrence County, Indiana. PHOTO BY SAMUEL S. FRUSHOUR.

surface-drainage basins that contain sinking streams, including the Lost River.

Streams having gradients less than the dip of the bedrock have eroded the bedrock surface of the Mitchell Plateau, resulting in its gently rolling topography. Those streams which still maintain their flow across the Mitchell Plateau have downcut through an east-facing escarpment and are incised into the Crawford Upland, which is developed on and into a series of interbedded shales, limestones, and sandstones of late Mississippian period, Stephensport, West Baden Group, and Blue River Group (fig. 6). The escarpment is known as the Springville Escarpment (formerly Chester Escarpment in Indiana) and is equivalent to the Chester, or Dripping Springs Escarpment, located east and south of Mammoth Cave in Kentucky, but it is somewhat different lithologically and structurally (DesMarais et al. 1973).

The Mitchell Plateau is a low limestone plateau, dissected by a few deeply entrenched streams such as the Ohio River, Buck Creek, Indian Creek, Blue River, Lost River, East Fork White River, Salt Creek, and its major tributary, Clear Creek (from south to north, respectively). North of the East Fork White River the plateau-like character of the Mitchell Plateau is lacking owing to deeply entrenched surface drainage patterns (DesMarais et al. 1973). North of the East Fork White River, a few square miles of well-defined sinkhole plain lie west of Bedford and Avoca in Lawrence County. Small isolated sinkhole areas can also be found in Owen, Morgan, and Putnam Counties.

The high-density sinkhole character of the Mitchell Plateau is evident as a wide zone along the western margin of the sinkhole plain where the soils have been removed by sapping, slumping, and piping into the underground channels and enlarged fractures. The eastern margin of the Mitchell Plateau, characterized by surface drainage, is covered by thick, somewhat impermeable soils ranging generally from 10 to 100 feet in thickness. This thickness of surficial material far exceeds the amounts of insoluble residues derived from the dissolved limestones and may be the result of residues left behind as the Springville Escarpment was eroded and retreated westward. The karst features found in profusion on the Mitchell Plateau are generally less frequent on the ridge tops lacking limestone in the Crawford Upland; however, karst features are found in the karst valleys or blind valleys and the flanks of ridges where limestone crops out (DesMarais et al. 1973). The karst valleys are former surface stream courses, possibly equivalent to the Blue River strath and Mitchell Plateau (Powell 1964), and are small karst plains within the Crawford Upland. Karst valleys in the Crawford Upland may have dry stream beds (*dry beds*) that carry water only from heavy precipitation or snow melt.

The water from some springs high on hillsides flows a short distance before sinking into the top of the limestone that is located beneath dry beds.

Some of the caves that collect surface water from sinkholes on the Mitchell Plateau generally drain westward down the bedrock dip beneath the Springville Escarpment to emerge as springs in the entrenched surface stream valleys of the Crawford Upland. The most notable of these are Harrison Spring near Blue River in Harrison County, and the Orangeville Rise and the Rise of Lost River in Orange County.

The through-flowing major streams across the Mitchell Plateau and the Crawford Upland were apparently entrenched during Tertiary time. Additional entrenchment occurred during early Pleistocene time because of the lowering of sea level and regional uplift of the central United States. Development of karst features and caves was initiated and intensified in the Mitchell Plateau and within limestone-floored valleys and ridges of the Crawford Upland during early to late Pleistocene time (Powell 1964).

Continued downcutting and scouring by major streams during the Illinoian age and pre-Illinoian stages of glaciations by glacial meltwater deepened the valleys with caverns formed at successively lower levels. Multilevel cavern development can readily be observed in caves such as Wyandotte Cave, Donaldson Cave, and Bluespring Caverns. During late Wisconsin and Illinoian glacial stages, the stream valleys acted as glacial sluiceways and were filled with glacial outwash to as much as 50 feet above present river levels. Original river channels are as much as 120 feet below present river levels. As a result of stream filling, low-elevation caverns were submerged and

Figure 28. Generalized stratigraphic column that includes bedrock in southeastern Indiana. MODIFIED FROM THOMPSON AND SOWDER (2006). Most southeast Indiana caves are found in rock of the Muscatatuck Group and the lower half of the Salina Group. Brackets define bedrock where caves may be found.

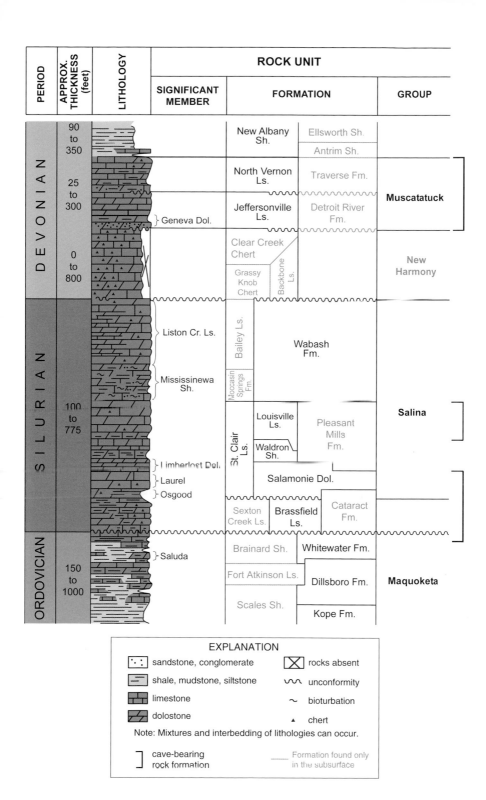

created alluviated cave springs where subterranean drainage routes could still maintain groundwater flow. Stumphole Spring at a bridge over the East Fork White River east of the town of Williams and Harrison Spring north of White Cloud are alluviated cave springs.

THE SOUTHEASTERN KARST AND CAVE AREA

The number, size, and complexity of caves formed in carbonate rocks of the Mitchell Plateau and Crawford Upland is greater than that of the southeastern karst and cave area developed on the Muscatatuck Plateau in parts of Clark, Decatur, Jefferson, Jennings, Ripley, and Switzerland Counties (fig. 4). A small region of till plain in Bartholomew County should also be included in the Muscatatuck Plateau. The southeastern karst and cave area has a broad swath of gently westward-dipping carbonate rock ranging in age from upper Ordovician to middle Devonian rocks exposed at the bedrock surface, although a mantle of glacial drift covers the uplands of the area. Great thickness of carbonate rock like that in the Mitchell Plateau and Crawford Upland is missing, but the more than 100 feet of limestone and dolomite is thick enough to contain some long caves (DesMarais et al. 1973).

Most of the caves in the southeastern part of the state are found in the Muscatatuck Plateau in the bedrock of Silurian and Devonian age (fig. 28). The ground surface slopes westward about half as much as the dip of underlying rock layers, so beds of younger rock are exposed to solution as one travels westward. Most of the southeastern caves and springs are found along stream valleys that are incised into the bedrock while sinkholes are found in isolated areas where glacial drift has been removed by erosion.

Visiting Commercial (or Tour) Caves

For the explorer who wishes some degree of comfort, there are a number of commercial caves that provide an enjoyable underground experience. One can view the corridors, streams, speleothems, and other wonders for the cost of a tour and the indulgence of a paid guide. A truly thrilling experience can be had without the crawling and scrambling necessary with undeveloped or wild caves. In Indiana, the tour cave experience is varied. As with any cave in the state, one must be dressed for a cool climate that is approximately 53°F. A light jacket or sweater is desirable and, because tour caves require walking on rocky or steep uneven trails, sturdy shoes are recommended.

Bluespring Caverns

Bluespring Caverns is the northernmost of the commercial caves and contains over 20 miles of underground streams in canyonlike passageways. It is located in Lawrence County just off U.S. Highway 50, about 5 miles southwest of the city of Bedford. On the tour, about 4,000 feet of stream passageway is viewed by boat; a wild cave tour for groups is offered during the colder months. Bluespring Caverns drains approximately 18 square miles of the Mitchell Plateau. Ridges that are part of the Crawford Upland also contribute water to this large cave system (fig. 29a). It is a very dynamic cave with flowing streams actively modifying their channels.

The entrance of this cave is a true collapse sinkhole where the soil and bedrock bottom of a pond collapsed in March 1940. A week later, young Janet Colglazier and a neighbor Bob Chenoweth climbed down tree roots into the opening and discovered a stream gurgling along in a large passageway. Knowing they would be in trouble for going into the cave, it was several weeks until they admitted to their parents what they found.

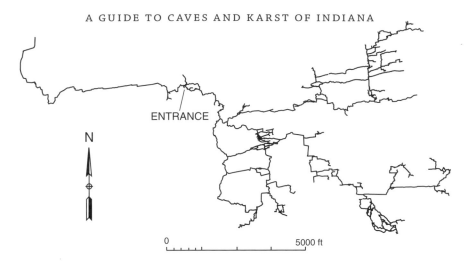

ENTRANCE

N

0   5000 ft

Figure 29a. Map of Bluespring Caverns in Lawrence County.
MAP BY SAMUEL S. FRUSHOUR.

However, these youths were not the first to see this underground river. Prior to a hydroelectric dam being built during
1911 and 1912 at the town of Williams in Lawrence County, local
residents occasionally paddled small boats a few hundred feet
into a tall canyonlike passageway at the spring exit of the cave.

Today an inclined trail into the sinkhole entrance ends at
the subterranean boat dock. There visitors view stream rapids
where the large cave stream heads off into blackness for over
a mile to eventually emerge on the East Fork White River. A
boat tour goes in the opposite direction, upstream past large
flowstone masses and stalactites (fig. 29b). Much of the tour
route is a high, canyonlike corridor with water-sculpted walls
and occasional mud banks. Eyeless fish and crayfish (plate 3) are
found throughout the boat route and the occasional washed-in
surface creature may be observed. Three-quarters through the
tour is a large rock nearly blocking the stream. This "Rock of
Gibraltar" is a stone that demonstrates how rock can separate
from the cave wall or ceiling once water has carved a very wide
passage beneath it. A natural bridge and the underside of a large
sinkhole are at the end of the tour. The cave stream continues

Figure 29b. The principle stream passage in Bluespring Caverns.
PHOTO BY SAMUEL S. FRUSHOUR.

beyond the tour route via a passage where the ceiling is only inches above the stream's surface. Beyond this point, the stream passage continues to the far reaches of this long cave and its numerous tributary underground streams.

Bluespring Caverns offers a tour for the more adventurous during the fall and winter months. This is a wild cave tour for youth groups who wish to climb and crawl into out-of-the-way places and camp within the cave.

UPPER TWIN CAVE AND DONALDSON CAVE

Spring Mill State Park is located along Highway 60 about 3 miles east of the town of Mitchell. The 1,319-acre park surrounds the upper section of a valley of Mill Creek that carries water northward to the East Fork White River. Spring Mill State Park is situated in the Mitchell Plateau where sinkholes count in the hundreds per square mile (fig. 30). Subterranean drainage from the sinkhole plain emerges at eight springs or spring caves in

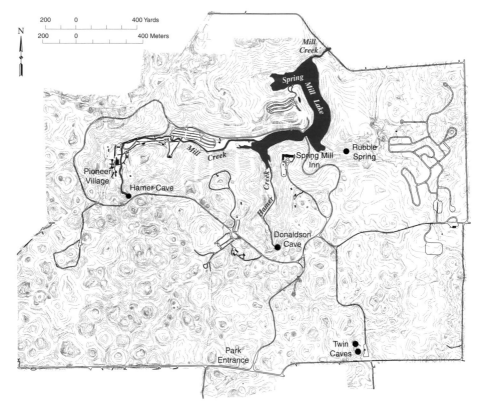

Figure 30. Topographic map of Spring Mill State Park in Lawrence County. MODIFIED FROM HASENMUELLER ET AL. (2003). Spring Mill State Park is in a high-density sinkhole region of the Mitchell Plateau. Donaldson Cave and Upper Twin Cave are popular public sites within the park.

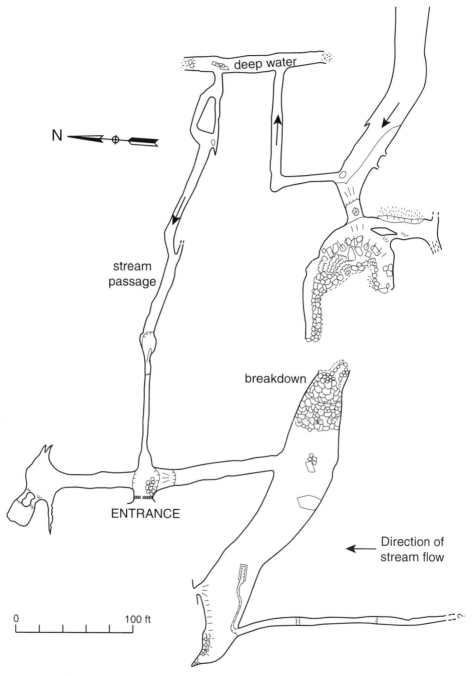

deep water

N

stream
passage

breakdown

ENTRANCE

Direction of
stream flow

0   100 ft

Figure 31a. Map of Donaldson Cave system in Spring Mill State Park,
Lawrence County. MAP BY MICHAEL MOORE (UNPUBLISHED).

Figure 31b. Donaldson Cave is situated at the head of a picturesque valley in Spring Mill State Park. Photo by Samuel S. Frushour.

the valley. Water from Hamer Cave powers the historic grist mill in the Spring Mill Village, while the stream of Donaldson Cave (fig. 31a) provides scenic beauty with cascades and riffles (fig. 31b).

Upper Twin Cave (fig. 32a) is a long cave that receives drainage from the sinkhole plain south of the park. A 400-foot-long boat ride takes visitors on the stream passage within the Salem Limestone. There are few speleothems in this cave, but of interest are the rock walls with undulations caused by uneven solution of the cross-bedding in the limestone and a scalloped texture that is dramatic in the light of lanterns. In the usually placid stream, eyeless fish and crayfish are seen. The collapse sinkhole between entrances of Upper and Lower Twin Caves is a classic example of a karst window (fig. 32b).

Downstream from the Upper Twin Cave and Lower Twin Cave entrances is another karst window at Bronson Cave which contains the same stream as Upper and Lower Twin Caves. The cave spring entrance of Donaldson Cave (fig. 30b) is actually the same cave as Bronson Cave and the same stream, as in Bronson

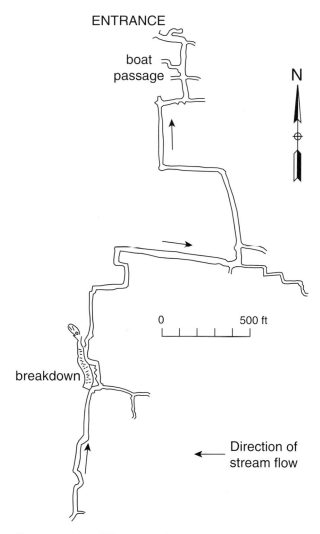

ENTRANCE

boat
passage

N

0   500 ft

breakdown

Direction of
stream flow

Figure 32a. Map of Upper Twin Cave in Lawrence County.
MODIFIED FROM POWELL (1961).

Cave, issues from it. The Donaldson Cave spring outlet is an
underground opportunity for visitors to explore the cave without special permission. A walkway above the stream inside
Donaldson Cave entrance leads visitors to an upper level aban-
doned long ago by the cave stream. Two hundred feet inside,
the underside of a collapse sinkhole is seen as a jumbled rock

Figure 32b. The entrance of Upper Twin Cave in Spring Mill State Park is in a karst window. The stream is the same as that which issues from Donaldson Cave. PHOTO BY SAMUEL S. FRUSHOUR.

choke sloping upward to the ceiling. Farther along the passage is a small windowlike hole to the outside world where one can look down upon the stream as it issues from the cave. A short distance from this hole is a side passage that can be followed far enough for visitors to feel like cave explorers. The experience of stoop walking and wading in the small stream may educate visitors as to whether they might enjoy exploring wild caves.

MARENGO CAVE

Marengo Cave is located in Crawford County on the east side of the town of Marengo just north of State Road 64. Discovered in 1883 and opened for public view in the same year, Marengo Cave (fig. 33a) has never ceased to delight visitors. Two tours of Marengo Cave are available, both of which are walking excursions through passages lined with speleothems. A third tour for the more adventurous in another entrance of Marengo Cave is in Old Town Spring Cave, which has a gaping spring entrance in the town of Marengo.

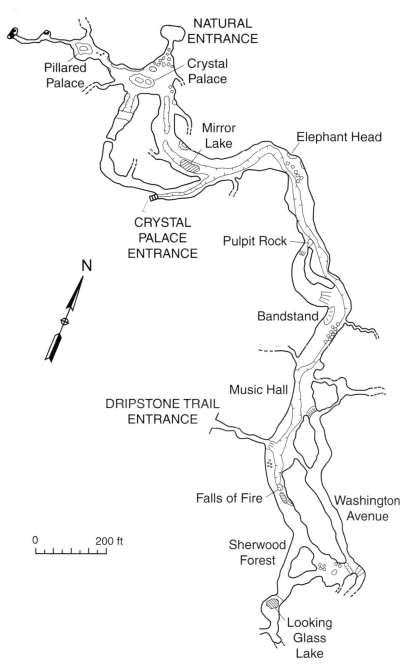

NATURAL
ENTRANCE

Pillared
Palace

Crystal
Palace

Mirror
Lake

Elephant Head

CRYSTAL
PALACE
ENTRANCE

Pulpit Rock

N

Bandstand

Music Hall

DRIPSTONE TRAIL
ENTRANCE

0   200 ft

Falls of Fire

Washington
Avenue

Sherwood
Forest

Looking
Glass
Lake

Figure 33a. Map of Marengo Cave in Crawford County.
MAP COURTESY OF MARENGO CAVE.

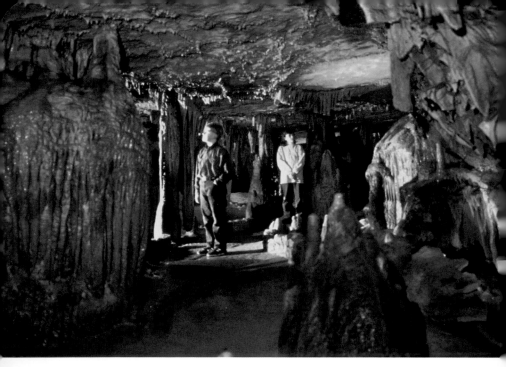

Figure 33b. Within Marengo Cave is the Crystal Palace, one of the points of interest on the public tour. PHOTO COURTESY OF MARENGO CAVE.

The original stream that flowed through the passage on each walking tour has been pirated into a separate lower passage (not shown on the map) that exits the cave as a spring west of the Visitors Center. This cave stream passage carries water from a 600-acre blind valley that is located 1½ miles to the north, where the runoff of precipitation flows into a large swallow hole cave entrance.

The Crystal Palace Tour enters the cave near the gift shop and proceeds by way of a large corridor with reflecting pools for about 500 feet to the well-decorated Crystal Palace (fig. 33b). Massive speleothems cover walls and rise from the floor as columns. Large stalactites abound on either side of the winding trail (Story of Marengo Cave undated).

The Dripstone Trail Tour is entered via an excavated entrance opened in 1979. As visitors enter the cave, they encounter the same large passage that is seen on the Crystal Palace Tour, but located about 800 feet south of that tour route. Numerous speleothems are encountered in the southwestern part of the cave at the Falls of Fire and Washington Avenue. The largest section of the main passage is at the Music Hall where the ceiling is 23 feet above the visitor's head and the passage is more than 50 feet wide. The cave tour finally exits the cave via the entrance for the Crystal Palace Tour.

SQUIRE BOONE CAVERNS

Squire Boone Caverns (fig. 34a) is located on the east bank of Buck Creek between Corydon and Mauckport in Harrison County. In the early 1800s, Squire Boone, a brother of Daniel Boone, migrated northward across the Ohio River from Kentucky to find new land and financial opportunity. At a steep head along Buck Creek a few miles from the Ohio River, he found a cave spring with a seemingly never-ending supply of water for the mill he intended to construct. He operated a grist mill for many years and when he died he was buried in a nearby small cave where he had once hidden from hostile Indians (Conway 1994).

The subterranean drainage of Squire Boone Caverns is similar to that of Spring Mill State Park and Cave River Valley Park, where precipitation infiltrates into the Mitchell Plateau and into bedrock of the St. Louis and Salem Limestones. Groundwater emerges in the cave as a steeply graded stream that eventually emerges as a spring near the head of a valley. The stream on the surface of the ground soon joins Buck Creek, the local base-level stream of the area.

Explorations into the cave and up a waterfall by cavers during the 1950s revealed a large passageway lined with speleothems of all shapes and sizes. The cave became known as a photographer's dream and home movie footage was shot in the cave in 1958. Local cavers developed it as a showplace for the public in the early 1970s.

The mill has been reconstructed and two artificial entrances have been excavated into the cave for the convenience of

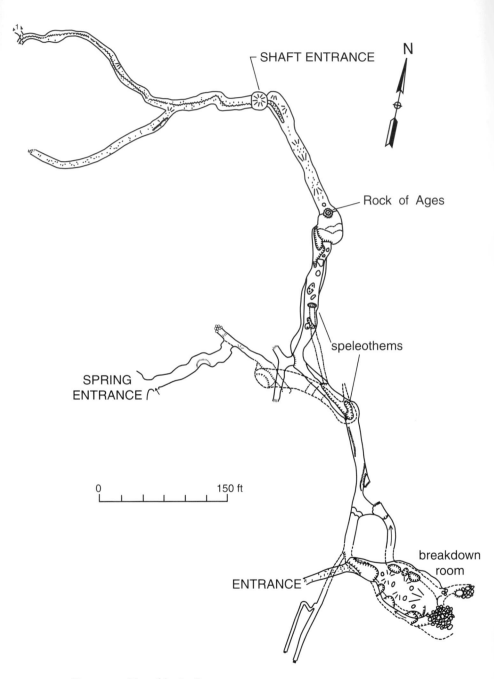

SHAFT ENTRANCE

N

Rock of Ages

speleothems

SPRING
ENTRANCE

0   150 ft

breakdown
room

ENTRANCE

Figure 34a. Map of Squire Boone
Caverns in Harrison County.
MAP BY DAVID DESMARAIS.

Figure 34b. The Rock of Ages column in Squire Boone Caverns, Harrison County. PHOTO BY SAMUEL S. FRUSHOUR.

visitors. Upon entering the cave, one finds dozens of delicate rimstone dams and an impressive bridge connecting the upper and lower levels of the cave. Most of the tour follows a cascading stream that leaves the tour route by plunging into a dark abyss and into a lower passage that leads to the spring exit. Visitors walk past delicate stalactites and among massive flowstone to a large rimstone dam, and overlook a giant column called the "Rock of Ages" (fig. 34b). This feature is viewed impressively from a high vantage point before walking beside it. The trail then takes the visitor back to the ground surface by ascending a spiral staircase installed in an excavated shaft of glistening wet limestone walls.

WYANDOTTE CAVE

Wyandotte Cave (fig. 35a) is located in Crawford County ½ mile north of State Road 62, about 11 miles west of Corydon and 4 miles east of Leavenworth and has a long history of recognition and exploration. Broad ridges in the eastern part of the Crawford Upland contain numerous caves as well as some of the long caves of Indiana. The cave was known to pioneers as early as about 1798, although ancient peoples visited this spacious cave as early as 4,100 years before the present (Munson and Munson 1990). Late Archaic and Early Woodland time period peoples mined chert, epsomite (Epsom salts), and aragonite from deep within the cave. Large quantities of snow-white aragonite were quarried from the base of the "Pillar of The Constitution" in the Senate Chamber located about 3,000 feet from the entrance. The remains of hickory bark torches and charcoal litter the sites of their excavations. Nineteenth-century explorers found the footprints of earlier visitors and mined Epsom salts from the cave as well. At the Junction Room, aboriginal peoples mined chert nodules from the limestone walls and left chips of chert when the nodules were struck to remove unwanted material. Artifacts made from Wyandotte Chert and white aragonite have been found in archeological sites hundreds of miles from the cave

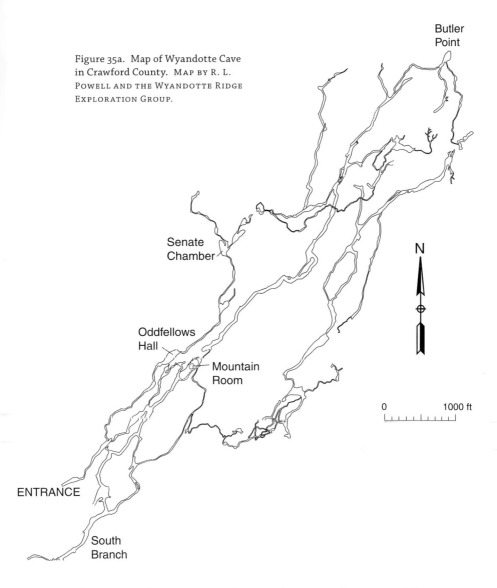

Figure 35a. Map of Wyandotte Cave in Crawford County. MAP BY R. L. POWELL AND THE WYANDOTTE RIDGE EXPLORATION GROUP.

Butler
Point

Senate
Chamber

Oddfellows
Hall

Mountain
Room

N

0   1000 ft

ENTRANCE

South
Branch

(Munson and Munson 1990). Wyandotte Cave became widely known during the War of 1812 because saltpeter-bearing earth was extracted from it for the making of gunpowder, although the majority of the local saltpeter production was probably at nearby Saltpeter Cave.

By 1850, visitors were paying to see the underground wonders; the discovery of additional large passageways (fig. 35b) in

Figure 35b. A large dry passageway along the tour route in Wyandotte Cave, Crawford County. PHOTO BY SAMUEL S. FRUSHOUR.

the same year added to the fame of the cave and increased the number of visitors (George 1991).

A variety of tours are offered depending on the time of year but the wild cave or *spelunking* tours for groups must be scheduled in advance. The Monument Mountain Tour is offered from May to August, and there is a historical tour that is also available during this time. Points of interest for the visitor are the large rooms and lengthy, dry passageways. The Crater Room, Queen's Palace, and Rothrock's Cathedral (fig. 35c) have stalactites, stalagmites, and flowstone speleothems. Along the tour route in the Discovery of Forty One are dozens of twisted or knotted helictites.

LITTLE WYANDOTTE CAVE

Little Wyandotte Cave is a few hundred feet around the hillside and south from Wyandotte Cave (fig. 36a). Although discovered around 1850, the cave was not shown to the public on a regular

Figure 35c. Monument Mountain and Rothrock's Cathedral in Wyandotte Cave. PHOTO BY SAMUEL S. FRUSHOUR.

basis until 1947 (George 1991). Electric lights and steel stairways were installed at that time to make visitation safer than the harrowing climb down into and then across a pit.

Entry is gained through a gate at the north entrance where speleothems are immediately encountered. The cave is well decorated with numerous stalactites and columns. Little Wyandotte surpasses the nearby larger cave for the sheer beauty of the different speleothems (fig. 36b). Not far into the cave, a clear pool of water is encountered that is accented by a large cone-shaped stalagmite. Farther on, the trail opens into a room that overlooks a gaping pit with massive flowstone and columns high on the wall. Beyond this overlook, a flight of steps descends to the top of a deep chasm carved by the action of downward-moving water.

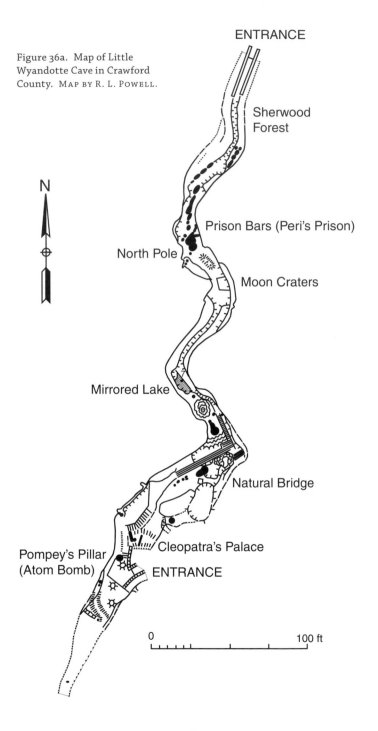

ENTRANCE

Figure 36a. Map of Little
Wyandotte Cave in Crawford
County. MAP BY R. L. POWELL.

Sherwood
Forest

N

Prison Bars (Peri's Prison)

North Pole

Moon Craters

Mirrored Lake

Natural Bridge

Cleopatra's Palace

Pompey's Pillar
(Atom Bomb)

ENTRANCE

0   100 ft

Figure 36b. Columns and stalagmites on the tour route of
Little Wyandotte Cave. PHOTO BY SAMUEL S. FRUSHOUR.

Beyond the chasm is a walkway up a steep slope on breakdown and flowstone. A few feet off the trail to the right a hole
goes downward. The tour guest will not wish to venture into this
small and muddy opening, but it winds down through precari-
ous-looking breakdown blocks and finally intersects the wall of
a cave passage. Zigzagging downward along the wall, a person
must squeeze through a couple of narrow openings and finally
climb down a small solution dome to get to the bottom where a
small stream disappears under the wall in a low crawlway. The
route down has been in a lower portion of the passage on the
tour route. This passage is the same one as the entrance passage
of Wyandotte Cave across the valley a few hundred feet away.
Downcutting of the valley, by erosion, between Wyandotte and
Little Wyandotte Caves has truncated a large cave passage creating two separate caves.

At the south part of Little Wyandotte, near another entrance, collapse and influx of soil have blocked the cave passage

and further progress through the cave. Approaching the south entrance of the cave, one sees a hole in the ceiling; this is the original entrance pit that visitors climbed down to gain access to the cave. The two new entrances were dug to allow easier access.

EXPLORING WILD CAVES

Entering any cave, especially a wild cave, visitors may experience strange feelings, and this is to be expected. You have entered a cave or underground environment that is completely different from life on the surface of our planet. Because humans are not well adapted to encounter the difficulties and delicate environment of the cave, we must learn how to explore without damaging the cave or ourselves. Some cave systems have interconnecting passages that may extend for miles, but most caves in Indiana are short—less than 1,000 feet long—and may contain streams. The dampness, an occasional bat, and unusual mineral formations (speleothems) can be unfamiliar. While many cave passages are small and must be crawled through, visitors may also encounter awe-inspiring vast spaces.

Caves seem eternal and many have been around for hundreds of thousands of years, but expanding human population and technology have brought a new generation of threats: pollution, vandalism, quarrying, and erosion of ground surface soil that fills passageways. Not every cave consists of a walking-sized passage or *borehole*. Many wild caves have passages that may be canyons filled with vigorous streams, tight fissures, small crawlways, natural bridges, waterfalls, pits, and domes. The obstacles within caves and the small size of many caves are why they are infrequently visited, and why they are not open to the public as commercial caves (Sira undated). Other factors that make caves uncomfortable are the dampness of walls and mud banks, humidity, and temperature. Most caves have nearly constant temperature year-round. That constant temperature is usually the average temperature on the surface of the ground above the cave—normally 53°F to 54°F in Indiana. The humidity is usually greater than 90 percent, which makes for very damp conditions. Because all surfaces are damp or even very wet and the temperatures are low, caves can be uncomfortable.

Figure 37. Basic minimum caving equipment includes hard hat with headlamp, sturdy boots, cave pack, knee pads, and gloves.
PHOTO BY JOHN DAY.

Caving is not necessarily a high-risk activity, but in certain situations with particular conditions, it can be extremely dangerous. The level of risk involved in caving is, to a very large extent, related to the risk-taking behavior or ignorance of the participants. It can also be affected by a wide variety of conditions that may be found in a cave. For the most part, caving accidents result from a combination of a lack of training, lack of proper equipment (fig. 37), lack of information, lack of preparation, and poor judgment. The Boy Scout motto "Be Prepared" especially applies to caving. Above all, exercising good judgment should reduce the level of risk when caving.

Being aware of possible hazards should help the cave visitor avoid them. Caving as a whole has a better safety record than many active outdoor sports. But above all, when visiting a cave, one must respect and protect the cave while exercising caution. Falls are by far the most common type of caving accident. Slow down and watch where you are stepping. Running, jumping, and other fast movements lead to increased risk of injury. An incapacitating injury can require a major rescue effort to bring out an injured person. Test handholds and footholds before committing yourself to your next move where there is possibility of falling. Some climbs require a safety rope, or belay, controlled by a companion. Free-climbing a rope, hand over hand, is foolish and most likely will result in serious injury or death. It cannot be done safely and should be discouraged. Vertical training from a competent vertical caver is necessary before attempting a climb in a cave.

Be aware that loose rocks may fall while caving. Avoid unstable breakdown (fallen rock) and steep rocky slopes. Standing under anyone who is climbing places the caver in danger of being struck by falling rocks or cave equipment. Stay off to the side of any climber who is above. When climbing, secure all loose gear to prevent dropping something on someone below. If even a small rock or piece of gear is dislodged or dropped, warn those below by shouting "ROCK!" loudly and clearly.

Some caves have active streams running through them and are subject to flash flooding during rainstorms or rapid snow melt. These occurrences can trap or even drown cavers. Flooding of cave passages has resulted in five of the seven deaths in Indiana caves since 1961. It is always wise to check the weather forecast before entering a wild cave. If you are in doubt about the potential for a cave to flood, postpone your trip or visit a different cave.

While traveling through a cave, narrow crevices and tight places may be encountered. Avoid forcing the body into places one cannot back out of, or where companions cannot assist the stuck person.

Getting lost in a cave can happen but there is little excuse for it. Becoming lost usually occurs because the cavers did not commit to memory what the cave looks like as they traveled along. Frequently look behind to see what the cave will look like on the way out and pay special attention to visualizing what junctions of passages look like. If lost, and there is no hope of reconstructing how to leave the cave, stay where you are and get as comfortable as possible. Conserve electric lights by turning them off for long periods. Stay alert for someone searching for you and call out occasionally to alert rescuers. A whistle carried for the purpose of signaling will help save the voice for thanking those who will spend hours searching for you.

Always leave word with a reliable person as to what cave you will be visiting and your expected time of return. Leave a margin of extra time, as most cave trips take longer than planned. Any rescue (and especially an unnecessary one) results in bad publicity and strained relations with cave owners.

A lack of adequate light can be extremely dangerous. Any caver stranded because of light failure should be very embarrassed, to say the least. That caver is now immobilized in total darkness until help arrives, which could be many hours. Every caver should carry at least three sources of light. The primary source should be attached to the hardhat or helmet (fig. 37). All sources of light should be durable and able to get you out of the cave. Spare batteries and extra bulbs are required to make a light source reliable. For comfort and safety, food and drink may be very important to provide energy depending on the number of hours you plan to spend in the cave, but be sure to take all leftover food and trash out with you (Sira undated).

Caving can be extremely physically demanding. You should be in reasonably good shape. A person in poor condition will tire quickly, slow the group, and ultimately shorten the cave trip. Know your limits and do not attempt caving beyond your capabilities. Beginners should start with short cave trips and work up to more challenging ones. Consult with an experienced caver if there are doubts about the demands of a particular cave trip.

Serious medical conditions or a chronic disorder such as heart disease, epilepsy, claustrophobia (fear of enclosed places), or acrophobia (fear of heights) are counter to safe caving practices. If inflicted with such conditions, do not go caving. It will put you and others with you in jeopardy.

Drugs and alcohol and caving create a dangerous situation. In a caving situation, a person must be mentally alert. These substances are likely to be looked on as something dangerous and unpopular with those whose cave trip the substance user is surely going to spoil.

SAFE CAVING PRACTICES

The following list of safe caving practices is meant to help beginning (and remind experienced) cavers, that there is nothing that will replace using good common sense. This publication cannot cover every conceivable situation encountered while caving, and additional reading on the subject is encouraged (Sira undated).

Follow these guidelines:

1. Always go caving with other people; never go alone.
2. Carry three sources of light.
3. Wear a good-quality hard hat with a chin strap and a primary light source attached.
4. If all lights fail, sit down and wait for help to come.
5. Always leave information with someone about which cave you are going to and your expected time of return, allowing several hours for unexpected delays.
6. Wear suitable rugged clothing and footwear.
7. Follow the lead of the more experienced caver or the person who knows the cave well.
8. Avoid jumping, since cave floors are seldom level; even a short jump may result in injury.
9. Practice rope work under the guidance of an expert before doing any vertical caving.
10. Caving can be extremely tiring; know your physical limits and watch for signs of fatigue in others.
11. Never go caving if you are in ill health or if you have a chronic disorder such as heart disease or epilepsy.
12. Carry a small first aid kit and a large trash bag to make a heat tent using the heat from a candle or carbide lamp.

13. If an immobilizing injury occurs, treat for shock (keep the injured person warm). If self-rescue of a person is not safe, contact local cave rescue personnel or the state police.
14. Sitting still can cause shivering after a period of time (the first symptom of hypothermia); so get moving and initiate activity.
15. The slowest caver sets the pace; the leader should go only as fast as others can follow.
16. If thoroughly lost in a cave, panic is the worst enemy. Remain calm, conserve your light; if you followed the rule about leaving word, you should have little to worry about.

If you are interested in finding out more information about caves and caving, check the organizations that are listed in appendix II.

Endless Cave

Endless Cave is located in Cave River Valley and administered by Spring Mill State Park personnel. Cave River Valley is located 3½ miles north of the town of Campbellsburg in Washington County (fig. 38a). It was originally known as Dry Clifty Cave and is one of several caves in the area. A trail leads to the cave from a small covered bridge spanning the stream that issues from River Cave (originally known as Wet Clifty Cave), the site of a pioneer grist mill. The large spring entrance of Endless Cave is approximately 17 feet high and 20 feet wide (fig. 38b). About 80 feet inside is a skylight entrance, and from there the visitor can walk about 1,200 feet before stooping and crawling are required. About 1,200 feet into the cave is a canyonlike side passage that is approximately 800 feet long and is considerably smaller than

Figure 38a. Map of Endless Cave, Washington County.
Courtesy of Bloomington Indiana Grotto.

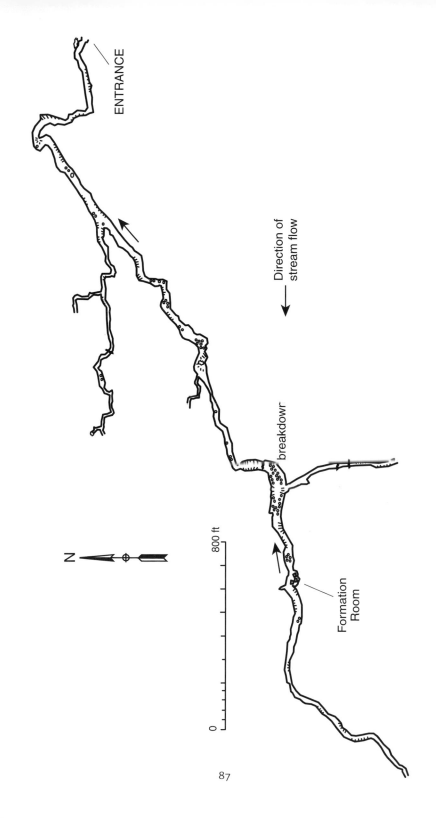

ENTRANCE

Direction of
stream flow

breakdown

Formation
Room

N

800 ft

0

Figure 38b. The entrance of Endless Cave in Cave River Valley, Washington County. PHOTO BY SAMUEL S. FRUSHOUR.

the main stream passage. There is a small fault on the wall just below the ceiling in one of the breakdown rooms far into the cave. The Mt. Carmel Fault is only a few hundred feet east of the cave, but this one small, sympathetic fault is the only obvious evidence that the larger fault is nearby. Endless Cave and other caves in the same valley drain a part of the Mitchell Plateau. These caves have formed by eastward-flowing water travelling down the dip of a syncline. The combined water from several caves flows as Clifty Creek north and to the East Fork White River in valleys that have dissected the Mitchell Plateau and Norman Upland.

RIVER CAVE

The stream flowing through Cave River Valley originates at the spring entrance of River Cave (fig. 39a). A small dam impounds the stream in the cave (fig. 39b) and ensures that the visitor gets soaked, but by carrying a small boat up the rocky streambed

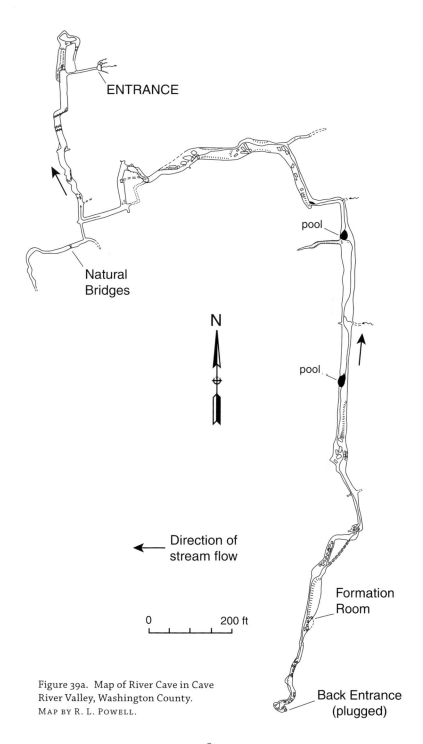

ENTRANCE

pool

Natural
Bridges

N

pool

Direction of
stream flow

0   200 ft

Formation
Room

Figure 39a. Map of River Cave in Cave
River Valley, Washington County.
MAP BY R. L. POWELL.

Back Entrance
(plugged)

Figure 39b. Water issuing from River Cave at Cave River Valley Park.
PHOTO BY SAMUEL S. FRUSHOUR.

to the cave, the visitor may be able to avoid swimming in the
54° water. Traveling into the cave beyond the dam, the stream
extends from wall to wall and the passage makes right-angle
bends. Large mud banks are eventually encountered and can be
traveled for about 800 feet. The passageway is blocked by collapse where a former entrance exists that is now choked with
rock and organic debris.

PORTER'S CAVE

A small area of sinkhole plain is present in Owen County (fig. 4)
about 6 miles north of the town of Gosport. Near the head of a
deep valley that intrudes into this sinkhole plain is a waterfall
and stream that issues from a magnificent spring cave opening. Numerous nearby sinkholes contribute drainage to the cave
system. Water is also contributed via a large swallow hole that
that is the terminus of a streambed where water comes from an

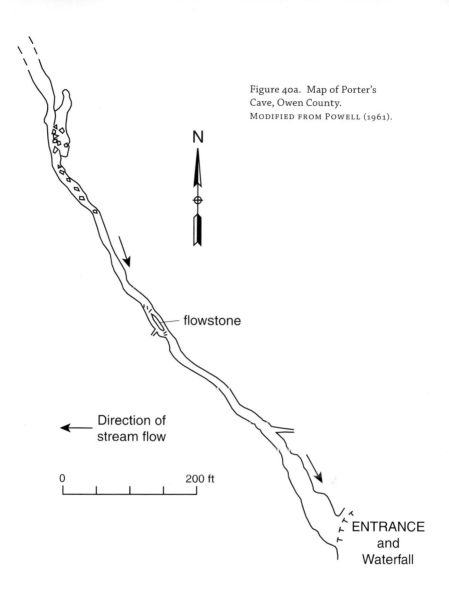

N

flowstone

← Direction of
stream flow

0   200 ft

ENTRANCE
and
Waterfall

Figure 40a. Map of Porter's
Cave, Owen County.
MODIFIED FROM POWELL (1961).

area once occupied by glacial Lake Quincy. Continental glacial
ice overran the area during the Illinoian glacial period where
Porter's Cave is now situated. As the ice melted and its southern
extent moved northward, a large lake and natural spillway was
created. Water flow from the lake and later from glacial meltwater of Wisconsin age scoured a new valley southward along
Limestone Creek (Wood et al. 2007). Water flow along the valley

Figure 40b. Entrance of Porter's Cave, Owen County, and large waterfall issuing from it. PHOTO BY JOHN DAY.

encountered limestone along the southern edge of the lake bottom. With time, increasing amounts of water were progressively captured by the enlarging underground conduits that formed Porter's Cave (fig. 40a).

Looking out over the valley from the entrance, one cannot help but be inspired by the vastness and beauty of the scene. A broad stream drops nearly 40 feet from the cave opening and cascades along the valley below (fig. 40b). Walking into the cave, the visitor must soon stoop over but only for a short distance. The passage opens into a tall, 8-foot canyon as it intersects a former higher stream channel on the right that terminates in mud fill. The main passageway continues straight ahead about 800 feet and throughout this passage there is a stream to wade through and occasional breakdown to scramble over. About midway along the stream passage the visitor may climb up and over a large flowstone that is developing below a small side passage.

WOLF CAVE

Wolf Cave (fig. 41a) is located within a small nature preserve along Trail 5 in the northern part of McCormick's Creek State Park. It has two entrances readily accessible from the trail and the visitor can enter one entrance (fig. 41b) and exit via the other without retracing one's route. It is not a large cave but annually provides scores of visitors of all ages with the real feel of a cave environment. Outside the smaller eastern entrance are the two Litton Natural Bridges, or Twin Bridges, which were formerly a part of the cave but rock collapse has isolated them from the rest of Wolf Cave. The cave is nearly dry in the summer months and provides the experience of walking, then stoop-walking, and

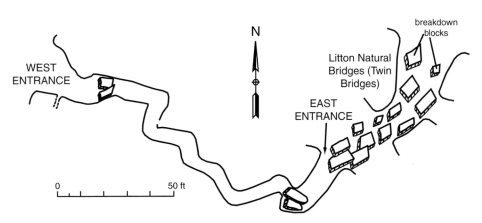

Figure 41a. Map of Wolf Cave in McCormick's Creek State Park, Owen County. COURTESY OF G. T. REA.

Figure 41b. Western entrance of Wolf Cave in McCormick's Creek State Park, Owen County. PHOTO BY JOHN DAY.

finally hands-and-knees crawling for long enough that many people find the cave memorable.

Along the trail to the cave are found a number of deep sinkholes that indicate groundwater is enlarging fractures beneath the ground surface. Proceeding to the vicinity of the western cave entrance, it is evident that erosion is lowering the surface terrain with ongoing deepening of the valley. As the valley deepened over time, water intersected bedrock joints or fractures resulting in subsequent development of the cave. Surface drainage in the valley no longer goes down valley beyond where the cave is located, and all drainage flows into the cave.

LANGDON'S CAVE

Langdon's Cave (fig. 42a) is located in O'Bannon Woods State Park south of Blue River. Permission to enter the cave and specific directions can be obtained at the park office on Indiana Highway 262 south of Highway 62. A small sinkhole entrance to

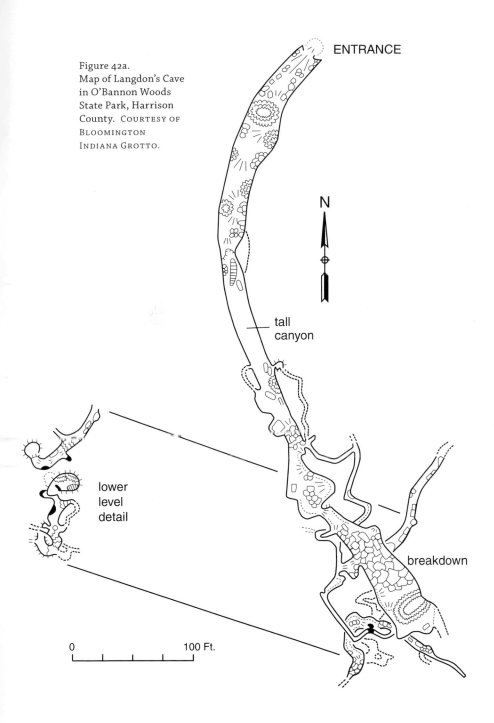

ENTRANCE

Figure 42a.
Map of Langdon's Cave
in O'Bannon Woods
State Park, Harrison
County. COURTESY OF
BLOOMINGTON
INDIANA GROTTO.

N

tall
canyon

lower
level
detail

breakdown

0   100 Ft.

Figure 42b. The entrance of Langdon's Cave, Harrison County.
PHOTO BY JOHN DAY.

Langdon's Cave (fig. 42b) leads to a tall canyon where the visitor must scramble down huge breakdown blocks and then walk with the ceiling sometimes 30 feet overhead. After traveling the floor of the deep canyon, large blocks of breakdown must again be climbed to continue to the end of the main passage. The cave consists of a large passageway that was truncated by valley downcutting at the entrance and at the farthest extent one can travel. As the hillside above was eroded away and sandstone protecting the cave was removed, water seeped downward along joints creating speleothems and also a series of pits that extend well below the floor of the large main passageway. Most of the cave is easily traveled with only an occasional pool of water in the main passageway to wet one's feet.

E. Y. GREEN CAVE

Located in the Crosley State Fish and Wildlife Area, E. Y. Green Cave (fig. 43a) is found along the creek north of the Area E parking lot and west of the high-tension power line. The scenic entrance is in a limestone cliff (fig. 43b) about 70 feet from the nearby stream. A much smaller cave is located in the same cliff a few feet to the west. The small area of sinkholes south of E. Y. Green Cave is the probable source of the small stream that intermittently flows from the entrance. The entire cave is a canyon

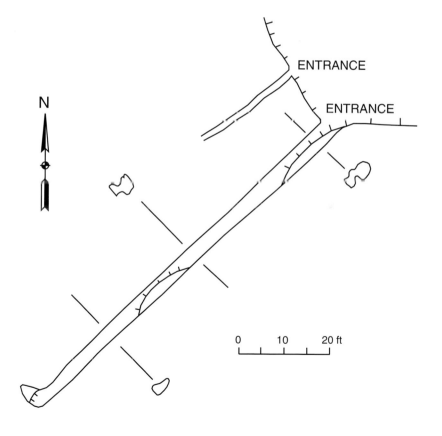

Figure 43a. Map of E.Y. Greene Cave in Crosley State Fish and Wildlife Area, Jennings County. MAP BY SAMUEL S. FRUSHOUR.

Figure 43b. The canyon passageway of E.Y. Greene Cave, Jennings County. PHOTO BY JOHN DAY.

approximately 5 to 8 feet high and 1 to 4 feet wide that is easily traveled. Jutting ledges and rock projections ensure that the visitor is in nearly constant contact with the walls.

BAT CAVE

Bat Cave is located in Versailles State Park just below the top of a bluff near Trail 2. It is a small cave that tests one's fervor for exploration (fig. 44a). The two small entrances were once a

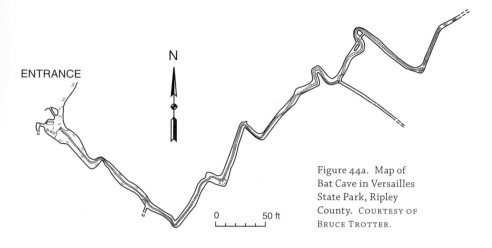

ENTRANCE

N

Figure 44a. Map of
Bat Cave in Versailles
State Park, Ripley
County. COURTESY OF
BRUCE TROTTER.

0   50 ft

spring exit for the water that formed the cave. The entrances lie
at the base of a 10-foot-high cliff (fig. 44b) and at the start of
a small erosion gulley running directly downhill to the valley
floor. The intermittent stream in the cave appears as a spring
just downhill from the entrances during wet weather.

Figure 44b. The entrance of Bat Cave at the base of an outcrop,
Ripley County. PHOTO BY SAMUEL S. FRUSHOUR.

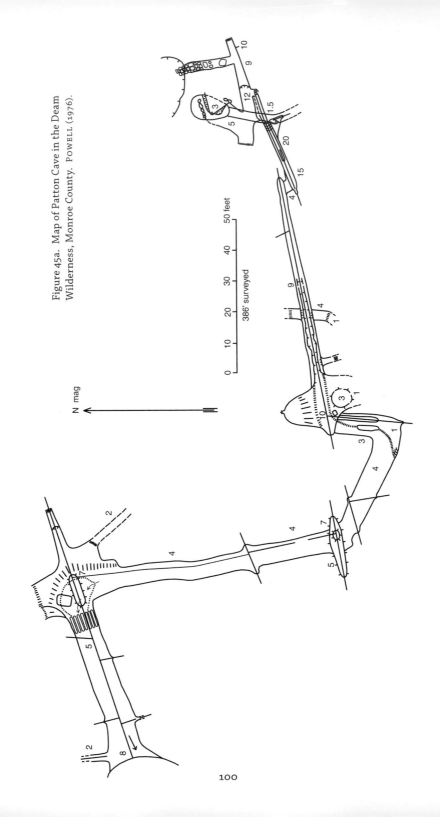

Figure 45a. Map of Patton Cave in the Deam Wilderness, Monroe County. POWELL (1976).

N mag

386' surveyed

0   10   20   30   40   50 feet

Throughout the cave, crawling is required because the highest part of the passageway is only 5 feet tall in one small area of the cave. Only a few feet inside the entrance, the small wet-weather stream sinks. The stream channel is then followed upstream throughout the main passageway while the explorer passes mud banks and flowstone. There is more than 700 feet of crawlway-sized passage, so knee pads are a welcome addition to the explorer's equipment.

PATTON CAVE

Located in the Deam Wilderness of the Hoosier National Forest, Patton Cave (fig. 45a) is one of a few remarkable caves located within the Norman Upland near the Mt. Carmel Fault. Access to the cave is either via boat on Lake Monroe or by hiking north from the Blackwell Horse Camp on Tower Ridge Road. There are

Figure 45b. Looking out of the nearly tubular entrance passageway of Patton Cave, Monroe County. PHOTO BY SAMUEL S. FRUSHOUR.

two entrances; the upper entrance is a swallow hole at the downstream end of a small blind valley. The larger second entrance is a spring entrance (fig. 45b) at the head of a valley overlooking the Saddle Creek inlet of Lake Monroe. One can walk into the spring entrance about 90 feet before crawling is required to reach the rest of the cave. Beyond the hands-and-knees crawl is a canyon-shaped passage with a short side passage. There are only a few speleothems, although wildlife such as salamanders and bats are sometimes seen. The cave remains fairly dry during the summer months when water rarely enters the upper entrance.

THE ETHICAL AND LEGAL ASPECTS OF VISITING WILD CAVES

The very act of passing through a cave chamber or passageway will cause a change to a cave. Microbes and lint are transported on clothing; even a well-placed footstep leaves a mark on an otherwise pristine cave floor. The considerate visitor will avoid walking where no one has previously stepped and will touch only rock that will not be blemished by doing so. There are a number of caves in Indiana that have suffered horrible disfigurement by vandals stealing the speleothems or leaving trash and body waste. Some caves now have muddy hand prints and boot markings where a few years ago a narrow trail of human footprints was the only evidence that people had been there. Some other caves show the thoughtless onslaught of mindless or ignorant speleothem bashing; the broken remains are scattered as if someone took great delight in being needlessly destructive (Sira undated).

The scribing of symbols or one's name in a cave will be of no interest to others and only ruins the cave experience for other people. There is no good reason to leave anything on cave walls or rocks and, of course, the best thing that can be taken away from the cave is the memory of pleasant scenery and the physical exhilaration felt by exploration.

Indiana has enacted statute IC-35-43-1-3 intended to protect caves, their features, and wildlife from harm. The statute reads:

Section 3. (a) As used in this section:
"Cave" means any naturally occurring subterranean cavity, including a cavern, pit, pothole, sinkhole, well, grotto, and tunnel whether or not it has a natural entrance.
"Owner" means the person who holds title to or is in possession of the land on or under which a cave is located, or his lessee, or agent.
"Scientific purposes" means exploration and research conducted by persons affiliated with recognized scientific organizations with the intent to advance knowledge and with the intent to publish the results said exploration or research in an appropriate medium.
(b) A person who knowingly and without the express consent of the cave owner:
(1) Disfigures, destroys, or removes any stalagmite, stalactite, or other naturally occurring mineral deposit or formation, or archaeological or paleontological artifact in the cave, for other than scientific purposes;
(2) Breaks any lock, gate, fence, or other structure designed to control or prevent access to a cave;
(3) Deposits trash, rubbish, chemicals, or other litter in a cave; or
(4) Destroys, injures, removes, or harasses any cave-dwelling animal for other than scientific purposes; commits a Class A misdemeanor.

LIABILITY OF LAND OWNERS

Farmers and other landowners often ask about their liability if they allow cavers on their property. Many rural people are proud of their woods and fields and do not mind sharing their outdoors with friends and neighbors. At the same time, they are afraid of the financial burden that could result if an injury resulted in a lawsuit. In the present legal climate, no one can feel entirely free of the possibility that a lawsuit may result. The best intentions of a person accidentally injured could be reversed by relatives seeking monetary compensation.

Indiana has adopted a law known as the Recreational Land Use Statute (IC14-2-6-3) to aid landowners. It eliminates liability for injuries caused as a result of the condition of the land, and it prevents monetary recovery initiated against the landowner for injuries to third parties that are caused by acts of a recreational user. The statute excuses an owner from liability to individuals (other than business invitees and invited guests) using the property for recreational purposes without monetary payments. The statute reads:

> Section 3. Any person who goes upon or through the premises including, but not as a limitation, lands, caves, waters, and private ways of another with or without permission to hunt, fish, swim, trap, camp, hike, sightsee, or for any other purpose, without the payment of monetary consideration directly or indirectly on his behalf by an agency of the state or federal government, is not thereby entitled to any assurance that the premises are safe for such purpose. The owner of such premises does not assume responsibility for nor incur liability for any injury to person or property caused by an act or failure to act of other persons using such premises. The provisions of this section shall not be construed as affecting the existing case law of Indiana of liability of owners or possessors of premises with respect to business invitees in commercial establishments nor to invited guests nor shall this section be construed as to affect the attractive nuisance doctrine. Nothing in this section contained shall excuse the owner or occupant of premises from liability for injury to persons or property caused by the malicious or illegal acts of the owner or occupant.

Afterword

Nearing the end of preparation of this book, bats in the northeastern United States were found to have contracted a fungus that caused them to terminate their hibernation in caves early to search for food. With no food available in winter, bats have died in great numbers. The fungus has spread rapidly since the malady was first discovered in 2006. Tens of thousands of bats have died from White Nose Syndrome. Although it is recognized that the White Nose Syndrome is spread from bat to bat in caves and bat to bat along normal migration routes, there is concern that people may be able to carry the fungus from cave to cave on shoes and clothing. Because of this great concern, federal and state agencies have temporarily closed caves on their properties to visitation.

In Indiana, all caves on the Hoosier National Forest are closed to visitation and all but one cave on Indiana state property is closed. A number of caves on private property are closed to visitation because they are major Indiana bat hibernacula. Of the tour caves, those privately owned are open to the public. These include Bluespring Caverns, Marengo Cave, and Squire Boone Caverns. Upper Twin Cave in Spring Mill State Park is open to visitors during summer months. We can only hope that White Nose Syndrome runs its course and bat populations recover or a remedy is discovered. Please observe mandated cave visitation closures until such time as the closures are reversed.

ACKNOWLEDGMENTS

There is a rich history of exploration and scientific study of caves in Indiana, from Timothy Flint, John Collett, Horace C. Hovey, William S. Blatchley, Archibald R. Addington, J. W. Beede, Preston McGrain, and Clyde A. Malott. Later investigators and explorers Richard L. Powell, Arthur N. Palmer, Louis Lamon, Leo Schotter, John L. Bassett, Carroll Ritter, Kevin Komisarick, David DesMarais, David Black, and Danny Dible, among many others, paved the way for recent explorers and scientists, and present and future cave surveyors. From this wealth of past contributions, current researchers and explorers have a solid base of information available to study known caves and to find new caves.

This publication would not be possible without the encouragement and assistance of Barbara Hill and Kimberly Sowder, whose persistence kept me on track during preparation. A special thanks to Julian J. Lewis and Salisa L. Lewis, who generously provided the section of cave fauna. To Richard L. Powell and John L. Bassett, whose wisdom often guided my writing, and to the many cavers who have generously provided ideas and knowledge, I am forever grateful.

Appendix I
Descriptions of Bedrock Associated with Caves

Mississippian Rocks

Stephensport Group

Glen Dean Limestone. This is a skeletal (fossiliferous) thick-bedded limestone, 9 to 31 feet thick, that typically includes blastoids, bryozoans, and brachiopods. In locations where it is present, it may be found beneath the Tar Springs Formation but is often unconformably beneath the Pennsylvanian sandstone of the Mansfield Formation. Several caves are formed in this limestone in Martin County.

Hardinsburg Formation. The formation is a soft, gray, carbonaceous shale and very fine-grained ripple-bedded sandstone. It is 20 to 62 feet thick in surface exposures from central Greene County to the Ohio River. It unconformably overlies the Haney Limestone in most places (Shaver et al. 1986). Only a few caves are known to penetrate these rock units.

Haney Limestone. The formation is dominantly a biomicritic, or skeletal limestone, and dolomitic mudstone. The formation is 20 to 40 feet thick and contains abundant blastoids with some crinoid plates and columns. Few caves are found penetrating this rock unit.

Big Clifty Formation. The unit is composed of 3 to 14 feet of gray, fossiliferous shale and interbedded limestone with 3 to 10 feet of varicolored mudstone and siltstone below it. These two upper units make up the Indian Springs Shale Member. Below these units are 25 to 40 feet of thinly bedded fine-grained sandstone, and, in places, as much as 5 feet of black pyrite-rich shale at the base of the formation (Shaver et al. 1986). The Big Clifty Formation is important roof rock that overlies and provides water to caves and springs developed in the Beech Creek Limestone.

Beech Creek Limestone. The formation is typically a gray skeletal or fossiliferous and lime mudstone 8 to 33 feet in thickness. The lower third of the formation is characteristically darker in color than the upper two-thirds. Fossils included are large crinoid columns and brachiopods. Numerous springs and most caves in Greene County are located in the Beech Creek Limestone.

WEST BADEN GROUP

These units and younger rocks may be missing in places because of erosion and deposition of Pennsylvanian sandstone of the Mansfield Formation. The West Baden Group comprises the Elwren Formation, Reelsville Limestone, Sample Formation, Beaver Bend Limestone, and the Bethel Formation. The Elwren Formation consists primarily of sandstone but grades into thin-bedded mudstone and shale. The Elwren thickness ranges 20 to 60 feet (Rea 1992). The Reelsville Limestone is characteristically a single bed of sandy, skeletal limestone 2 to 7 feet thick, and its occurrence is erratic (Shaver et al. 1986). Vertical shafts that begin in these rock units extend downward into the Paoli Limestone, however. The Sample, Beaver Bend, and Bethel Formations typically are sandy enough that they lack significant solutional potential to facilitate horizontal dissolution processes.

BLUE RIVER GROUP

Paoli Limestone. This rock unit is the lowest part of the Chesterean Series of rocks and is characterized by four distinct lithologies which are considered members. In descending order, they are: (1) the Downey Bluff Member composed of gray to light-gray, medium-grained skeletal and oolitic limestone; (2) gray or greenish-gray calcareous shale and discontinuous beds of skeletal limestone and lime mudstone of the Yankeetown Member; (3) the Renault Member, consisting of gray to green-ish-gray skeletal to oolitic limestone and lime mudstone; and (4) gray calcareous sandstone, dark shale, and impure sandy limestone of the Aux Vases Member, which in some places grades without break into the overlying member. The thickness of this formation ranges from 20 to 35 feet throughout most of its outcrop (Shaver et al. 1986) and, along with overlying Chesterian rocks, produces numerous sinkholes, springs, pits, and cave entrances in the Crawford Upland.

Ste. Genevieve Limestone. The Ste. Genevieve Limestone is a formation of carbonate rock sequences that ranges from 45 to 220 feet thick, where it is deeply buried in the western part of the state. Most of the large cave passages under the eastern part of the Crawford Upland, including Wyandotte Cave, are located in the Ste. Genevieve Limestone, although the entrances to these caves are often in the overlying Paoli Limestone. Its beds are composed primarily of oolitic, lime mudstone, skeletal, and detrital limestone. Shale, dolomite, sandstone, and chert compose about 10 percent of the combined Paoli and Ste. Genevieve Limestones. The formation is divided into three prominent members: the Joppa, Karnak, and Fredonia. The fossiliferous Lost River Chert bed is usually prominent about 20 feet above the base of the Fredonia Member, which is also the base of the Ste. Genevieve Limestone. The upper contact with the Paoli Limestone is somewhat uneven but seems to represent only a minor depositional break (Shaver et al. 1986). The Bryantsville Breccia bed at the top of the formation is composed of fragments of lime mudstone or oolitic limestone cemented by calcite. The Bryantsville consists of one or more beds up to 12 feet thick. The Ste. Genevieve formation undoubtedly contains the most abundant enterable caves of any rock unit in Indiana.

St. Louis Limestone. The St. Louis Limestone can be informally divided into two parts on the basis of lithology. The upper one-eighth to one-third consists mainly of medium-to dark-gray-brown lime mudstone, pelletal, and skeletal limestone and very thin beds of medium-gray slightly calcareous shale. Nodules and thin, discontinuous beds of mottled gray chert are abundant in the upper 25 to 90 feet of the formation. The lower part of the formation is mainly pelletal lime mudstone and skeletal limestone, calcareous shale and siltstone, and dolomite. The formation is 70 feet thick in Putnam County but thickens erratically to about 150 feet in Washington County (Shaver et al. 1986). The lower part of the St. Louis Limestone is important to cave development in Spring Mill State Park and Cave River Valley Park and this formation could arguably be credited as the dominant karst-producing rock strata of the Mitchell Plateau. Caves, springs, and numerous sinkholes are found near the base of the St. Louis Limestone.

SANDERS GROUP

Salem Limestone. A world-famous dimension limestone, also known as Indiana Limestone and Bedford Stone, is used in buildings and monuments and has been quarried from part of this formation since 1827. The massive building stone deposits are often cross-bedded with medium to coarse fossil grains and colored tan, light tan, and gray. The individual grains are mostly broken and abraded micro-fossil fragments with a scattering of macro-fossils. The principal depositional environment was in carbonate shoals. The thickness of the unit ranges from 60 to 100 feet in a southward direction from Monroe County. The cave passages of Spring Mill State Park, Bluespring Caverns, and caves in Cave River Valley Park are partly developed in the building stone beds of the Salem Limestone. Cave passages in the Salem Limestone form as a result of solution by ground-water in conduits within overlying dolomite and limestone of both the upper part of the Salem Limestone and the overlying St. Louis Limestone.

Harrodsburg Limestone and Ramp Creek Formation. These rock units are generally composed of a well-cemented, skeletal limestone but they include some shale, dolomite, and lime mudstone. The Harrodsburg is up to 70 feet thick near the town of Harrodsburg, with thinning both to the north and south of Monroe County (Shaver et al. 1986). Several caves are located in the Harrodsburg Formation with one example being Patton Cave overlooking Lake Monroe at the Saddle Creek Inlet (Rea 1992). The Ramp Creek Formation is typically 0 to 45 feet thick sitting directly on the thick solution-resistant and noncave-producing siltstones of the Borden Group. The lower part of the Ramp Creek includes geodes and other silicified materials.

DEVONIAN ROCKS ASSOCIATED WITH CAVES

MUSCATATUCK GROUP

The approximate total thickness of this formation is 65 feet in the Muscatatuck River area of North Vernon and thins in a northeastern direction (Shaver 1974).

North Vernon Limestone. Although it is basically a limestone, the North Vernon has many variations of facies both laterally and vertically. The upper part of the formation is the Beechwood Member that consists of gray and dark-gray medium-grained to very coarse-grained crinoidal limestone that is thick-bedded. The limestone sometimes contains glauconite and at its base there may be black phosphate grains and pebbles. The two lower members of the formation consist of gray dense massive argillaceous dolomitic limestone called the Silver Creek Member and below it gray fossiliferous limestone that is granular to shaley and thin-bedded. This is the Speed Member. The formation conformably overlies the Jeffersonville Limestone in southeastern Indiana.

Jeffersonville Limestone. The Jeffersonville Limestone has three often distinct members and unconformably overlies rocks of Silurian age. The uppermost member is the Vernon Fork Member, which is approximately 17 feet thick in the vicinity of Vernon. Three different dolomites and limestone are found in this member. The characteristic lower variety shows cyclic sedimentation. A single cycle starts at its base as a medium-to-light-gray fine-grained dolomite containing some rounded quartz grains. This dolomite is massive to wavy irregular thin-bedded with some color change in the upper beds of the cycle. Color in the upper part of the cycle is medium-yellowish-brown to light-yellowish-brown and the rock is very fine grained (Shaver 1986).

The second variety of dolomite in the Vernon Fork Member is fine-to-medium-grained, vuggy and mostly brown. It is often absent in the southeastern part of the state. A third variety of carbonate rock in this member ranges from dolomite to nearly pure limestone. These rocks may be very strongly laminated and brecciated, and their striking appearance has given rise to the name "Laminated Beds of the Jeffersonville Limestone." Both the top and bottom parts of the Vernon Fork are marked by concentrations of rounded and frosted sand grains.

Geneva Dolomite Member. The rock of this member is usually a calcareous dolomite that is buff to chocolate brown in color, rather soft, granular, and vuggy. It also contains bands and partings of carbonaceous material. The Geneva Dolomite is massive to thick-bedded in its lower part and commonly thin-bedded in its upper part. The distinctive colors are largely because of a high organic content with the near-surface beds oxidized to pale tan, cream, or white. White cleavable crystalline calcite masses are scattered through the fine-grain dolomite matrix. Some calcite masses make up beautifully preserved identifiable fossil casts. Chert is sometimes present, and quartz sand is common in the basal rocks (Shaver et al. 1986).

The Geneva overlies the Dutch Creek Sandstone Member of the Jeffersonville Limestone in southwest Indiana; however, the Dutch Creek may not be present in the southeastern cave or karst area.

SILURIAN ROCKS ASSOCIATED WITH CAVES

As the result of erosion, an unconformity between Devonian and Silurian rocks exists in southeastern Indiana. It is possible that a small part of the Moccasin Springs Formation may be found in the Shelbyville area and further south. The Louisville Formation is usually found as the first identifiable rock formations below the unconformity.

Louisville Limestone. The Louisville Limestone is an argillaceous limestone that is approximately 60 feet thick near the Ohio River and may vary considerably in thickness owing to the uneven Devonian-Silurian unconformity. Near its base there is often a clastic transitional zone as the limestone grades into the Waldron Shale.

Waldron Shale. The formation is characteristically interbedded shale and limestone that overlies the Salamonie Dolomite. Shale is prominent with fossiliferous beds of limestone that become thin near the base of the formation. Overall thickness of the formation is 5 feet in the vicinity of the Ohio River but the thickness is variable and increases in an easterly direction (Shaver et al. 1986).

Salamonie Dolomite. In southern Indiana, the Salamonie is generally impure fine-grained argillaceous limestone and dolomitic limestone. The upper rocks in the formation are the Laurel Member. They are generally more pure carbonate and may have some vugs and chert present. Thickness of the formation may be 0 to 60 feet because of erosion and its unconformal relationship with the underlying Brassfield Limestone.

Brassfield Limestone. The Brassfield Limestone is generally a medium to coarse-grained fossiliferous limestone that has numerous irregular bodies and stringers of shale scattered throughout. In many places it contains Ordovician pebbles in the lower part. Small amounts of fine-grained dolomite are present in most sections of the formation. This formation is generally less than 4 feet thick along outcrops with a maximum thickness of 14 feet. The formation is absent in parts of Decatur, Jefferson, Jennings, and Ripley Counties (Shaver et al. 1986).

APPENDIX II
Cave-Oriented Organizations

American Cave Conservation Association
PO Box 409
Horse Cave, KY 42749
www.cavern.org

Bloomington Indiana Grotto
PO Box 5283
Bloomington, IN 47407-5283
www.caves.org/grotto/big/big.html

Central Indiana Grotto
PO Box 153
Indianapolis, IN 46206
cig.caves.org

Eastern Indiana Grotto
c/o Mark Webb
350 W. King Street
Franklin, IN 46131
www.caves.org/grotto/eig

Evansville Metropolitan Grotto
c/o Bob Sergesketter
1090 Hopf Avenue
Jasper, IN 47546-3822
www.caves.org/grotto/emg

Harrison-Crawford Grotto
c/o David L. Black
PO Box 147
Georgetown, IN 47122-0147
www.caves.org/grotto/hcg

Indiana Cave Survey
c/o David Everton
7240 Zikes Road
Bloomington, IN 47401-9261
www.caves.org/survey/ics/

Indiana Karst Conservancy
PO Box 2401
Indianapolis, IN 46206-2401
www.caves.org/conservancy/ikc

National Speleological Society
2813 Cave Avenue
Huntsville, AL 35810-4431
www.caves.org

Northern Indiana Grotto
Box 10297
Ft. Wayne, IN 46851-0297
www.caves.org/grotto/nig

Saint Joseph Valley Grotto
PO Box 3052
Elkhart, IN 46515
www.caves.org/grotto/sjvg

Western Indiana Grotto
c/o Doug Hanna
375 W. National Ave
Terre Haute, IN 47885

GLOSSARY
of Cave, Karst, and Geology Terms

The glossary is intended as a convenience to readers who encounter unfamiliar terms in this publication or in other publications on caves, caving, or karst.

ALABASTER Massive gypsum deposits; this term is sometimes also applied to calcite.

ALLUVIATED SEDIMENTS The process of sediment deposition by a stream.

ALLUVIUM Deposits of clay, silt, sand, gravel, or stones by relatively recent stream activity.

ANASTOMOSIS TUBES A network of small, interconnecting solution tubes along partings of bedding planes and joints. They may appear as inverted stream channels on the cave ceiling. They are the result of solution during the initial development of a cave passageway.

ANTHODITE A cluster of long crystals, usually aragonite, that radiate outward from a common base on the wall or ceiling of a cave passage.

ANTICLINE Upward arched bedrock layers resulting from uplift forces within the earth.

AQUIFER Subsurface rock strata or unconsolidated deposits that store and transmit or yield water in measurable quantity.

ARAGONITE A form of calcium carbonate ($CaCO_3$) with an orthorhombic, or needlelike, crystalline structure.

BACON A thin, draperylike sheet of calcite that has alternating dark and light bands giving the appearance of bacon. The dark stain is often an oxide of iron.

BASE LEVEL The generalized or hypothetical level below which streams may not deepen their channels by erosion.

BATHTUB A portion of a cave stream passage where the ceiling lowers close to the water surface forcing a person to become substantially immersed.

BED A deposit, or layer, of bedrock that lies between two well-defined boundary or bedding planes.

BEDDING PLANE A defined surface that separates one layer of rock from another.

BEDDING PLANE PARTING A separation between adjacent rock beds or along bedding planes.

BEDDING PLANE PASSAGE A cave passage that is considerably wider than it is high and that may meander. They are unlikely to have actually formed along bedding planes but usually began with solution along joints.

BLIND VALLEY A valley in which no water leaves the valley as a surface stream.

BLUE RIVER STRATH Valley floors within the Crawford Upland that are approximately equivalent to the erosion surface of the Mitchell Plateau.

BOREHOLE Large and easily traveled cave passages in which a person can walk upright.

BOTRYOID Calcium carbonate deposits in the form of grape-like nodules.

BOX WORK Deposits of calcium carbonate within fractures in the bedrock. Subsequent solution of the bedrock exposes a latticelike structure.

BREAKDOWN Rock that litters the cave floor that used to be part of the ceiling or walls. A pile of this rubble may also be called a *breakdown.*

BREAKDOWN DOME See breakout dome.

BREAKOUT DOME A more or less circular, dome-shaped cave room created by progressive rock fall.

BREATHING CAVE A cave or portion of a cave where air currents change direction at more or less regular intervals.

CALCITE Calcium carbonate ($CaCO_3$), the principal mineral in limestone and the material from which most stalactites, stalagmites, flowstone, and other speleothems are made.

CALCITE BUBBLE A rare form of calcium carbonate concretion that is hollow and rounded; found on the surface of water.

CALCITE RAFT Thin sheets of calcium carbonate that are precipitated and that float on the surface of still water.

CARABINER A more or less oval metal ring with a spring-loaded gate that opens inward. It is used for attaching ropes or slings to climbing equipment and as an aid in rope climbing and rappelling.

CARBONIC ACID A mild, naturally occurring acid (H_2CO_3) that occurs when rain or groundwater combines with carbon dioxide.

CAVE A natural underground passageway, recess, chamber, or series of chambers. The term *cave* may also be used as a verb to describe the process of collapse.

CAVE CORAL This is a catch-all term describing a variety of nodular, globular, botryoidal, or corallike speleothems usually composed of calcium carbonate. This term is also used for cave deposits that have formed under water.

CAVE ONYX Calcite or aragonite with stained bands of other minerals. It has a shiny luster when polished.

CAVE PEARL A roundish, unattached concretion of calcium carbonate formed by the tumbling action of falling mineral-laden water.

CAVER One who usually enters caves for scientific or other nonsport reasons. It has been said that cavers rescue spelunkers.

CAVERN In the United States, this term is used interchange-
ably with cave.

CHERT A dense, fine-grained form of silica that breaks with
a conchoidal fracture and sharp edges. It may appear nodular,
bedded, or as irregular lumps. It is sometimes referred to as
flint.

CHIMNEY (Noun) A narrow vertical shaft or slot in rock. It
may be a rough tube resembling a house chimney or a narrow
cleft between two rock walls. (Verb) To ascend or descend in a
series of body motions by pressing one's back against one wall
and pressing the feet against another wall.

CLASTIC ROCKS Rock derived from the disintegration of
other rocks where particles are mechanically transported deposited and consolidated. Examples are sandstone and shale.

COLLAPSE DOME See breakout dome.

COLLAPSE SINKHOLE A depression or sinkhole resulting
from the collapse of bedrock into a void or cave. Bedrock is
often exposed in the sides of the sinkhole.

COLUMN A speleothem formed by the growing together, or
union, of a stalactite and a stalagmite.

COMMERCIAL CAVE A cave that may have guides for the
convenience of paid visitors and improvements of the cave
that may include trails and lights.

COMPRESSION DOME See breakout dome.

CONCRETION A lump or nodule of mineral built of layers in
water or as a secondary deposit within bedrock. Chert (silica
dioxide) as a concretion may be prevalent in limestone.

CONDUIT A subterranean passage formed by solution that is
too small for humans to enter.

CORROSION The mechanical enlargement of cave passages
by the abrasive action of water-borne particles.

CRAWLWAY A cave passageway small enough that a person must be on the knees or on the stomach to pass through it.

CROSS BEDDING Layers of sediments deposited at an angle to and nonparallel to adjoining layers of sediments.

CUTTER See grike.

CUTOFF See subterranean cutoff.

DEAD CAVE A term incorrectly applied to a cave into which water no longer penetrates so that the speleothems are dry and not growing.

DETRITAL LIMESTONE Limestone made up of fragments of older disintegrated limestone.

DIP The angle at which a bed of rock stratum is tilted from horizontal.

DISSOLUTION The process of dissolving rock to create caves or karst landforms.

DIVIDE See drainage divide.

DOGTOOTH SPAR A variety of calcite crystal that forms where the crystal has a prominently displayed pointed end.

DOLINE Sinkholes of great size that are 30 or more feet across.

DOLOMITE A carbonate rock, often resembling limestone, in which more than 50 percent of the calcium has been replaced by magnesium to form calcium-magnesium-carbonate $(CaMg(CO_3)_2)$.

DOME A vertical shaft or room formed by rock collapse that projects upward from a horizontal cave passage.

DOME-PIT A vertical shaft or solution shaft that extends both upward and downward from a cave passage intersecting the shaft.

DOLOSTONE See dolomite.

DRAINAGE AREA See watershed.

DRAINAGE DIVIDE The rim or boundary between drainage basins or watersheds whether they are on the surface of the ground or underground in the vadose or phreatic groundwater zones.

DRAPERY A hanging speleothem (usually calcium carbonate) that takes a form resembling a curtain or pleated window drapery.

DRIPSTONE A general term for calcite deposits, or speleothems, formed by precipitation of minerals from water.

DRY BED (OR DRY STREAM BED) Stream beds that only occasionally carry floodwaters and are prominent karst features in areas of soluble bedrock.

DYE TRACE The process of introducing a fluorescent dye substance into a sinkhole or swallow hole and attempting to detect where dye and water reemerges after traveling underground.

EPIKARST The upper surface of soluble bedrock and near rock surface solution-enlarged fractures originating owing to aggressive acidic soil water. The feature is sometimes also called *near karst* or *exokarst.*

ESCARPMENT A steep erosion-formed slope that separates areas of flat or rolling terrain from a region of higher elevation. The slope angle remains more or less constant as the escarpment erodes or weathers moving in the direction of down the local bedrock dip.

FACIES The various aspects belonging to a geological unit of sedimentation, including mineral composition, type of bedding, and fossil content.

FAULT A rock surface or zone of rock fracture along which there has been displacement of the rock.

FEN See karst fen.

FILL Rock, sand, gravel, mud, or other material on the cave floor deposited by collapse or by running water.

FLINT See chert.

FLOATER Rock imbedded in soil and no longer attached to bedrock.

FLOWSTONE Calcite deposited where water is moving down a cave wall or over the floor.

FLUTE Vertical ridge or bladelike projections on cave or vertical shaft walls resulting from the downward motion of water.

FLUVIAL Pertaining to the action of rivers.

GLACIAL DRIFT All deposits of glacial origin.

GLACIAL SLUICEWAY Stream channels and streams that carry the load of sand and gravel from melting glaciers.

GLACIAL OUTWASH Sand, gravel, and rocks deposited by glacier meltwater streams.

GLACIAL TILL Unsorted and nonstratified glacial deposits.

GRADED FILL Rocks or other hard material used to fill and stabilize a sinkhole. The material grades from coarse at the bottom to fine at the top.

GRAPE FORMATION See botryoid.

GRIKE Linear soil-filled channels that are found in the upper surface of carbonate bedrock. They have no bedrock roof and in Indiana are usually associated with the Salem Limestone.

GROTTO American usage of this word refers to a cavity opening off a larger cavity. It is also the term used by the National Speleological Society for its suborganizations, rather than *chapter*.

GROUNDWATER All subsurface water in caves or fractures, or in pore spaces of bedrock or unconsolidated deposits.

GULF An elongated collapse sinkhole with steep walls and more or less flat floor that may have a stream emerging and then sinking. Several collapse sinkholes may coalesce to form this feature.

GYPSUM Hydrated calcium sulfate ($Ca(SO_4)+2H_2O$) that may appear in caves as bundles of needles, curved flowerlike crystals, or as crust on a wall. It is a common mineral within limestone.

GYPSUM CRUST Gypsum may crystallize over a large expanse of cave wall resulting in a sheet or crustlike feature.

GYPSUM FLOWER Crystalline gypsum crystals in a curved or twisted form resembling flowers. Gypsum migrates through bedrock and crystallizes at the air and rock interface.

HELICTITE A variant form of stalactite that does not hang vertically, but is wormlike or has side branches.

HYDROLOGIC CYCLE The complete cycle of phenomena through which water passes, beginning as atmospheric water vapor passing into liquid or solid form as precipitation, then along or into the ground, and finally returning to the form of atmospheric water vapor by means of evaporation and transpiration.

HYDROLOGY The scientific study of water movement and water chemistry on and in the earth.

ICE CAVE A cave formed entirely within a mass of ice by melting or a cave in bedrock in which ice forms and is retained for some time, even after temperature on the surface of the ground is no longer freezing. Such caves are sometimes referred to as cold traps.

INCISED STREAM A stream that has cut its channel deeper with little sideward movement of the channel.

INTERMITTENT STREAM A stream that may or may not have water depending on whether there has been sufficient precipitation for surface runoff. Also see dry bed.

JOINT A systematic fracture in bedrock that interrupts the physical continuity of a rock mass. In carbonate rocks, some joints may extend through several beds of rock (master joints) and have lengthy similar more or less parallel joints nearby, while other joints (cross joints) may transcend only one bed of rock and end at master joints, intersecting them at more or less right angles. Certain joints are not vertical but may be inclined at a high angle. The numerous fractures in bedrock often confuse the interpretation of joints.

KARREN Exposed bedrock pinnacles or ridges uncovered by erosion of residual soil. Also see lapies.

KARST (Classical definition) The term for a landscape characterized by sinkholes, sinking streams, lapies, springs, cave entrances, or absence of surface streams. These features indicate the presence of underground streams, conduits, and caves. The term is a German word derived from the Slav word *krs*, meaning craggy or rock. It refers to the area east of Trieste in the former Yugoslav Republic. (Modern definition) The modern definition of karst includes the classic karst landforms but also encompasses subsurface features in carbonate rocks which relate to the flow of groundwater. Some researchers have modified the classical definition of karst to include caves and the solution-modified joints or fractures in the limestone beneath a karst region. The definition is imprecise and evolving.

KARST AQUIFER A body of rock beneath a karst area that is sufficiently permeable enough to transmit groundwater and to yield significant quantities of water at springs and wells.

KARST FEN A shallow sinkhole wetland. These can be found in the eastern part of the Mitchell Plateau in Orange County.

KARST HYDROLOGY The study of water flow and water chemistry in soluble bedrock aquifers.

KARSTIC An adjective that implies a feature (such as limestone) is associated with karst features or karst terrain.

KARST SPRING Where groundwater emerges from natural underground cavities in a region of soluble bedrock.

KARST VALLEY An elongated valleylike feature containing karst features with no permanent surface streams entering or leaving it. Stormwaters sometimes exit these valleys in a stream bed that is usually dry.

KARST WATER Groundwater associated with karst features. Water is not a karst feature; however, the phrase is often used inappropriately.

KARST WINDOW A sinkhole feature resulting from the collapse of a cave roof where the cave passageways at each end of the collapse may be evident.

KEYHOLE PASSAGE A cave passage that resembles a canyon with the top portion widened so that the cross-section view of the passage is that of an old-fashioned keyhole.

LAPIES Mounds, pillars, or cones of carbonate bedrock that crop out on the surface of the ground.

LEAD An unexplored passage in a cave.

LIMESTONE A sedimentary rock consisting chiefly of calcium carbonate ($CaCO_3$) in the form of the mineral calcite.

LITHOLOGY The physical character or description of a rock generally determined by the unaided eye (such as coarse grained or microcrystalline).

MICRITIC LIMESTONE Limestone consisting of microcrystalline calcite; it is often described as lime mudstone.

MOON MILK A white, plastic, or pasty substance (when wet) or powder (when dry) that is often composed of a hydromagnesite mineral but can be of other mineral compositions. This substance is associated with particular forms of bacteria.

MUD CRACKS Fine-grained sediments shrink into plates separated by cracks as a result of moisture leaving the sediments.

MUD STALAGMITES Projections of mud similar in shape to calcite stalagmites but created by the repeated process of water drops falling and splashing mud into a small circular mound. Mud is then deposited in the water-drilled hole by subsequent flooding and water drops again splashing the mud, creating a higher mud projection.

ONYX See cave onyx.

OOLITIC LIMESTONE A variety of limestone composed largely of small spheres (oolites) of calcium carbonate.

OUTCROP The exposure of bedrock to the surface of the ground.

PALEOKARST Ancient karst features that have subsequently been buried.

PALETTE See shield.

PELLETAL LIMESTONE Limestone containing aggregates of calcite grains whose boundaries are often discernable only under polarized light.

PERMEABILITY The capacity or property of a rock, soil, or other material to transmit fluid. The velocity of the fluid is measured in centimeters per second or Darceys.

PENEPLAIN A nearly flat and nearly featureless landscape produced by erosion.

PHREATIC WATER Water that is contained within the phreatic zone.

PHREATIC ZONE The water-saturated region below the water table or potentiometric surface in bedrock. This is the region in the bedrock occupied permanently by groundwater.

PIPING The process where a tunnel or small conduit is developed in soil because of progressive sediment removal into underground voids by seepage of water. They may originate as small animal burrows or in association with plant roots.

PISOLITE See cave pearl.

PIT From the viewpoint of the observer, a vertical shaft looking down from its top. See vertical shaft.

PLATEAU A relatively flat or rolling region of land that is higher than a nearby ocean or major stream. There is less uniformity of topography than in the case of a plain.

PLEISTOCENE The epoch of time after the Tertiary that is known to have extensive continental glaciations in the United States; also the first of the two epochs of the Quaternary period.

POROSITY The percentage of a rock that is occupied by pore spaces, whether isolated or connected.

POTENTIOMETRIC SURFACE The theoretical level to which groundwater will rise to if it were not impaired by low permeability of the bedrock; usually measured in wells.

POTHOLE A hemispherical or bowl-shaped depression formed by falling water in bedrock streambeds. Also used in Great Britain and some European countries to describe a vertical shaft open to the surface of the ground.

PRUSIK The process of climbing a rope using ropes attached to the climber and to the standing rope via symmetrical fist-like knots.

PSEUDOKARST A landscape that has features similar to those found in karst landscapes, but is formed in relatively insoluble rocks by nonkarst-forming processes.

RAPPEL The various techniques of sliding down a rope in a controlled manner using a rappelling device attached to the body.

RELIEF The difference in elevation between the high and low points of a land surface.

RIMSTONE Calcium carbonate deposited from water in the form of a dam or latticework of dams.

RISE A spring in which water wells up more or less vertically from below.

ROCK FACIES See facies.

ROCK UNIT A stratigraphic unit or rock type defined by lithology or structure without regard for age or fossil record.

SAPPING Removal of soil from the soil-bedrock interface by the action of groundwater rising and falling in joints or fractures.

SCALLOP The more or less spoon-shaped hollows carved into bedrock by the action of eddies or turbulence in flowing water. The faster the flowing water, the smaller the scallops; the upstream curve of the scallop is steepest. This is useful for determining flow direction where a stream is no longer present.

SCOUR A depression in a stream bed created as the result of fast-flowing water.

SELENITE Gypsum crystals in the form of blades or bundles of needles.

SHAFT See vertical shaft.

SHELTER CAVE A deep overhang or depression in the face of a cliff.

SHIELD A speleothem of calcium carbonate that has formed in the shape of a disk jutting outward from the wall at an upward angle.

SHOW CAVE See commercial cave.

SINK See swallow hole; is also sometimes confused with *sinkhole.*

SINKHOLE A depression in the land surface that may be only a few centimeters or several kilometers across. Some have gentle side slopes and others may have vertical walls. They are indicators that subsurface drainage exists in a soluble bedrock region; however, not all areas of subsurface drainage have sinkholes.

SINKHOLE PLAIN A plain or nearly flat region on which most of the relief is due to sinkholes and nearly all drainage is subterranean.

SINKING STREAM A surface stream that loses water to the underground.

SIPHON Not a true siphon with an inverted U-shape, but a section of cave passage that is totally flooded to the ceiling.

SKELETAL LIMESTONE Limestone that owes its characteristics to in-place fossils or fossil fragments.

SLUMP PIT A hollow or hole in the sediments of a cave floor caused by solution or erosion of underlying rock, resulting in subsidence.

SODA STRAW A thin, tubular stalactite that resembles a drinking straw. Water travels only inside the tube and calcium carbonate is deposited out of a water drop on the end.

SOLUTION SHAFT See vertical shaft.

SPELEOLOGY The scientific study of caves using disciplines such as geology, biology, and various technical skills.

SPELEOTHEM Any secondary mineral deposit that is formed in a cave. Common forms include stalactites, stalagmites, flowstone, and columns. These are not karst features. The word *speleothem* replaces the term *formation,* which is more appropriately used to describe the grouping of several beds of rock.

SPELUNKER One who is inexperienced and explores caves solely for sport.

SPRING The place of outflow of water that has been underground in conduits, caves, or pore spaces.

SPRING ALCOVE This feature may appear as a notch or cutout in a valley slope at the site of a spring or former spring.

SQUEEZE A part of a passageway in a cave that is very tight for a human to pass through.

STALACTITE A calcium carbonate deposit that grows downward, iciclelike, as the result of water moving into the air on a cave ceiling or the underside of a ledge.

STALAGMITE A mound or projection deposit of calcium carbonate that is built upward in a cave by dripping water.

STEEP HEAD The steep or nearly clifflike slope above the emergence of a spring or former spring.

STRATA Plural of stratum.

STRATUM A series of bedrock beds that may be of similar composition or similar description.

STREAM TRACE See dye trace.

STRATIGRAPHY Descriptive geology pertaining to the character, age, sequence, and correlation of bedrock in a given area.

STRIKE The compass direction of a line at right angles to the dip in a rock deposit.

SUBTERRANEAN CUTOFF A surface stream abandons a section of surface channel for a shorter underground conduit. Water sinks in a swallow hole and reemerges as a spring farther downstream in the original surface stream channel.

SUMP A pool of water where the passage beyond is flooded.

SYMPATHETIC FAULT A usually diminutive fault that is adjacent to a larger fault and may exist as a result of the same fault-producing forces.

SYNCLINE Downward arched layers of bedrock as a result of forces within the earth.

SWALLET See swallow hole.

SWALLOW HOLE The opening or depression where a surface stream loses its water into the ground.

TERRAIN A region of the Earth's surface considered a single physical feature. Examples are sinkhole terrain, mountainous terrain, and ridge terrain.

TERRA ROSSA The red, clayey soil associated with regions having soluble bedrock and karst features. It is a product of the weathering processes that destroy carbonate bedrock and other forms of bedrock.

TERTIARY The earlier of the two periods comprising the Cenozoic era. Also the system of rock strata developed during that period.

TOPOGRAPHY The collective physical features of a region that may be represented on maps by contours and relief symbols.

TRAVERSE To cross a rock ledge or wall laterally. The term is also used as a noun.

TRAVERTINE A term loosely applied to the various forms of calcium carbonate deposits.

TROGLOBITE Animals that permanently live in caves. Cavers have sometimes been referred to with this term.

TWILIGHT ZONE The dimly lighted region inside a cave entrance that never receives direct sunlight.

UNCONFORMITY A bedrock surface modified by erosion prior to new deposition of sediments with the result that rock strata is missing from the depositional sequence.

VADOSE WATER Water moving by gravitational forces within the vadose zone.

VADOSE ZONE The bedrock region above the water base level or water table where water flow is influenced by gravity in partially water-filled caves, conduits, fractures, or pore spaces. This region may still be considered as vadose even though seasonal rises in water level may temporarily saturate it.

VERTICAL CAVING The act of traveling through a cave using ropes and rope climbing techniques.

VERTICAL SHAFT A vertical tube or conduit that is enlarged by the action of water running down walls. Initial development begins with water moving downward in joints or where joints intersect.

VUG A small cavity in a rock or vein, often with a mineral lining of different composition from that of the surrounding rock.

WATERSHED The area contained within a drainage divide where all water that enters is channeled out through a single exit such as a stream or spring.

WATER TABLE The upper surface of the zone of water saturation. In limestone regions, this surface may be irregular or nonexistent where bedrock exhibits low permeability. In bedrock of high fracture or conduit permeability, caves and fractures may be both above and below this surface.

WILD CAVE A cave in its more or less natural state where paths, lights, or other conveniences for the public have not been installed.

References Cited

Banta, A. M. 1907. The fauna of Mayfield's Cave. *Carnegie Institute of Washington Publications* 67: 1–114.

Bassett, J. L. 1974. Hydrology and geochemistry of karst terrain, upper Lost River drainage basin, Indiana. Master's thesis, Indiana University.

Conway, W. F. 1994. *The incredible adventures of Daniel Boone's kid brother—Squire.* 2nd ed. New Albany, Ind.: FHB Publishers.

DesMarais, D., G. Spaulding, B. Wilson, and M. Moore, eds. 1973. *NSS 73 Convention Guidebook.* Huntsville, Ala.: National Speleological Society.

George, A. I. 1991. *Wyandotte cave down through the centuries.* Louisville, Ky.: George Publishing Company.

Gray, H. H. 2000. *Physiographic divisions of Indiana.* Special Report 61. Bloomington: Indiana Geological Survey.

Hasenmueller, N. R., C. B. Rexroad, R. L. Powell, M. A. Buehler, and J. L. Bassett. 2003. *Karst geology and hydrology of the Spring Mill Lake and Lost River basins in southern Indiana.* Guidebook 15. Bloomington: Indiana Geological Survey

Hasenmueller, N. R., and R. L. Powell. 2005. *Karst: A distinct type of landscape or topography.* Poster 4. Bloomington: Indiana Geological Survey,.

Hill, C., and Forti, P. 1997. *Cave minerals of the world.* 2nd ed. Huntsville, Ala.: National Speleological Society, Inc.

Hill, J. R. 2004. *Summary of Indiana geology.* Bloomington: Indiana Geological Survey, CD-ROM.

Klimchouk, A. B., D. C. Ford, A. N. Palmer, and W. Dreybrodt, eds. 2000. *Speleologenesis evolution of karst aquifers.* Huntsville, Ala.: National Speleological Society.

Lewis, J. J., R. Burns, and S. L. Lewis. 2004. *The subterranean fauna of the Hoosier National Forest.* Final Report. Washington, D.C.: U.S. Department of Agriculture, Forest Service.

Malott, C. A. 1919. The "American Bottoms" region of eastern Greene County, Indiana: A type unit in southern Indiana physiography. Indiana University Studies 6 (40). Bloomington: Indiana University Press.

———. 1952. The swallow-holes of Lost River, Orange County, Indiana. *Proceedings of the Indiana Academy of Science* 61: 187–231.

Munson, P. J., and C. A. Munson. 1990. *The prehistoric and early historic archeology of Wyandotte Cave and other caves in southern Indiana.* Prehistory Research Series 7 (1). Indianapolis: Indiana Historical Society.

Palmer, A. N. 2007. *Cave geology.* Dayton, Ohio: Cave Books.

Powell, R. L. 1961. *Caves of Indiana.* Circular 8. Bloomington: Indiana Geological Survey.

———. 1964. Origin of the Mitchell Plain in south-central Indiana. *Proceedings of the Indiana Academy of Science* 73: 177–182.

———. 1970. *Karst development west of Bloomington, Indiana.* Memorandum Report. Bloomington: Indiana Geological Survey.

———. 1976. *Some geomorphic and hydrologic implications of jointing in carbonate strata of Mississippian age in south-central Indiana.* Ph.D. thesis, Purdue University.

Rea, G. T., ed. 1992. *Caving in the heartland: A guidebook for the 1992 convention of the National Speleological Society.* Huntsville, Ala.: National Speleological Society.

Shaver, R. H. 1974. The Muscatatuck Group (new middle Devonian name) in Indiana. Occasional Paper 3. Bloomington: Indiana Geological Survey.

Shaver, R. H., C. H. Ault, A. M. Burger, D. D. Carr, J. B. Droste, D. L. Eggert, H. H. Gray, et al. 1986. *Compendium of Paleozoic rock-unit stratigraphy in Indiana: A revision.* Bulletin 59. Bloomington: Indiana Geological Survey.

Sira, Adrian. n.d. *A guide to responsible caving.* Huntsville, Ala.: National Speleological Society.

The Story of Marengo Cave, undated brochure.

Thompson, T. A., and K. H. Sowder. 2006. *Generalized stratigraphic column of Indiana bedrock.* Poster 6. Bloomington: Indiana Geological Survey.

Wayne, W. J. 1949. A karst valley in western Monroe County, Indiana. *Proceedings of the Indiana Academy of Science* 59: 258–263.

Wood, J. R., S. L. Forman, and D. W. Everton. 2007. The extent and timing of a pre-late Wisconsin ice margin in central Indiana: A new view from glacial-lacustrine sediments from Porter Cave. *Journal of Cave and Karst Studies* 69 (3): 369.

INDEX

Numbers in italics refer to pages that contain illustrations.

For SAMUEL S. FRUSHOUR, the quest for knowledge about caves has been a 50-year journey into caves in the United States, Mexico, and the Caribbean. His favorite caves are in Indiana and Kentucky, and much of his effort has been spent there mapping and photographing them and assisting biologists and archeologists. As past head of the Field Services Section of the Indiana Geological Survey at Indiana University, he devoted more than 20 years to investigating karst features and caves and providing information about them to landowners, consulting companies, and government agencies.